Praise for

WOUNDED by God's People

Friendly fire. It's the term used to describe soldiers killed in the line of duty by their fellow fighters. In every war, the percentage of deaths attributed to this phenomena is shocking. Yet it pales in comparison to the number of human hearts that have been disparaged and broken by fellow believers — people who were supposed to be fighting with us not against us. In *Wounded by God's People*, Anne bravely and with vulnerability brings this issue to light and then gives us a solution; a salve to soothe the wounds of the offended. This book is a much-needed, long-anticipated tool that will change the future of the body of Christ.

        Priscilla Shirer, *New York Times* bestselling author
        of *The Resolution For Women*

It's important to talk about our wounds this honestly. Anne has done a beautiful job using the pain of her past to tell the story of a loving, healing, and redeeming God. This book is a testimony to a God who never gives up on us, never stops chasing us, and loves us more than we ever thought — even if His people don't.

        Kyle Idleman, author of *Not A Fan* and *Gods At War*

I so appreciate Anne writing these honest words about the deep hurts of being wounded … betrayed … rejected … and accused. I know these hard places personally. And it's doubly hard when it comes from within the body of Christ. But we don't have to just stew and suffer alone. With great wisdom and deep empathy, Anne has given all of us wounded warriors a place of sweet grace to turn to when we get knocked down.

        Lysa TerKeurst, *New York Times* bestselling author
        of *Made to Crave* and *Unglued*

Enemies cannot betray you. Only a friend can. And sometimes, that friend can emerge from your inner circle of closest confidants. It's why the wounds we suffer at the hands of other Christians always run deep and leave scars. Thankfully, my friend Anne Graham Lotz provides wise words of comfort and encouragement in *Wounded by God's People*, one of her finest works. She answers the prophet's age-old cry "Is there no balm in Gilead?" reminding us that Jesus restores, heals, and gives us the heaven-sent ability to forgive. I heartily recommend *Wounded by God's People* for *every* follower of Jesus!

Joni Eareckson Tada, Joni and Friends International Disability Center

Anne has written a deeply personal book. You will be moved by her transparency and vulnerability as she shares her most hurtful wounds, inflicted by those in the body of Christ. But ultimately, as the story of Hagar shows and Anne illustrates so eloquently, God is the Great Healer of your wounded heart.

Mark Batterson, *New York Times* bestselling author of *The Circle Maker*

Anne Graham Lotz has boldly taught God's Word and stood courageously for biblical principles. Even in the face of wounding criticism, she has never wavered in her convictions. There is no one I respect more than this godly woman.

Shirley Dobson

Anne's extraordinary new book encourages us to find our "inner Hagar" and set her free by the power of forgiveness. She has turned her own deep wounds into profound healing for others.

Kathie Lee Gifford

Wounded by God's People is a book that we have needed for a long time. I know so many people who have been hurt by the church — and too many have hit back. I left the church for years because of one comment one elder made about me. It was two decades before I came back. I highly recommend this love-saturated, Scripture-based, long-needed combination of straightforward teaching and poetry, both convicting and healing, rich and deep. I am ordering multiple copies.

Francine Rivers, bestselling author of the Mark of the Lion series

Ouch! It hurts to be maligned by some in the world who believe we Christ-followers are haters and bigots. But that pales in comparison to the hurt we feel from wounds inflicted by those who also purport to follow Jesus. Those are the deepest cuts. Anne Graham Lotz knows that pain full well. But she also knows where to go to bind those sharp wounds. Open this book and let Anne guide you to forgiveness and restoration as she shares the pain that she has known; that Hagar experienced; that, perhaps, you too have encountered. Let Anne walk you right to Jesus, for He too knew those wounds — and He can heal your pain.

Janet Parshall, nationally syndicated talk-show host

Why are we surprised when another follower of Christ wounds us? God's people — as all people — are broken beings who hurt others with our actions. Anne Graham Lotz brings good news to both the wounded and the wounding children of God: God redeems our pain through his own. By his wounds we are healed. Read and be restored.

Elisa Morgan, publisher, www.fullfill.org, speaker,
author of *The Beauty of Broken*, www.elisamorgan.com

When Christians cause harm to other Christians, there is often a ripple effect: you have the injury itself, then an inability to trust God's people, and then even an inability to trust God Himself. Anne Graham Lotz provides hope and transformation for this issue in her book. I highly recommend it.

Dr. John Townsend, leadership consultant and psychologist, coauthor of *Boundaries*

I love this book because it's wise, humble, and remarkably transparent. Whatever your pain, you will find that Anne Graham Lotz understands. With candor and grace, she offers the kind of help that may well heal your soul.

Ann Spangler, author of *Praying the Names of God*

Wounded by God's People is a remarkable book that sheds light on the devastating problem of being wounded and inflicting wounds within the Christian community. Speaking from experience, Anne brings clarity and understanding to those who have suffered through seasons of great loss. Insightful and authentic, she pulls back the veil on the darkness of betrayal by God's people and offers alternative, godly responses to the wounding that has been done.

Vonette Bright, cofounder, Campus Crusade for Christ, International

FOREWORD BY BETH MOORE

WOUNDED
by God's People

DISCOVERING HOW GOD'S LOVE
HEALS OUR HEARTS

ANNE
GRAHAM
LOTZ

ZONDERVAN®

ZONDERVAN

Wounded by God's People
Copyright © 2013 by Anne Graham Lotz

This title is also available as a Zondervan ebook. Visit www.zondervan.com/ebooks.

Requests for information should be addressed to:

Zondervan, *Grand Rapids, Michigan 49530*

Library of Congress Cataloging-in-Publication Data

Lotz, Anne Graham, 1948–
    Wounded by God's people : discovering how God's love heals our hearts /
Anne Graham Lotz.
      pages cm
    Includes bibliographical references.
    ISBN 978-0-310-26289-3
    1. Hagar (Biblical figure) 2. Healing—Religious aspects—Christianity.
3. Suffering—Religious aspects—Christianity. 4. Pain—Religious aspects—
Christianity. I. Title.
BS580.H24L68   2013
248.8'6—dc23
                                                       2013013057

Any Internet addresses (websites, blogs, etc.) and telephone numbers in this book are
offered as a resource. They are not intended in any way to be or imply an endorsement
by Zondervan, nor does Zondervan vouch for the content of these sites and numbers
for the life of this book.

Published in association with the literary agency of Alive Communications, Inc., 7680 God-
dard Street, Suite 200, Colorado Springs, CO 80920. www.alivecommunications.com

Cover design: Michelle Lenger
Cover photography: Don Farrall / Getty Images®
Interior illustration: iStockphoto®
Interior design: Beth Shagene

Printed in the United States of America

13 14 15 16 17 18 19 /DCI/ 21 20 19 18 17 16 15 14 13 12 11 10 9 8 7 6 5 4 3

Dedicated
to
the wounded

Contents

Drawn from a Well 11
  Foreword by Beth Moore

Jesus Understands 15
  He Was Wounded Too

Healing Is a Journey 21
  You Are Invited to Begin

The Biblical Story of Hagar 25

1. Loved by God on the Periphery 29
   God Is Not an Elitist

2. Life Is Hard 43
   Everyone Is Wounded

3. The Cycle of Pain 53
   The Wounded Become Wounders

4. The Believer in Exile 67
   Running from the Wounders

5. God Cares 77
   You Can't Outrun God

6. Spiritual Blind Spots 89
   You Are Missing the Obvious

7. Wounding Hurts 103
   Doing the Right Thing Can Be Painful to the Wounder

8. Rejected by Them 119
   But Not by Him

9. Wandering in the Wilderness.......................129
   God Is Still There

10. God Stands By 139
    He Hears Your Cry for Help

11. The Silence Is Broken 151
    God Is a Prayer-Hearing, Prayer-Answering,
    Miracle-Working God

12. A Stubborn Spirit.....................................163
    Exile from Him Is Self-Imposed

13. The Turning Point.....................................171
    That Was Then, This Is Now

14. I Can See! 181
    Your Valley May Be the Place of Vision

15. Don't Look Back.......................................191
    You Can't Move Forward by Looking in the Rearview Mirror

16. It's Time to Move On 207
    You Can Be Reconciled

Conclusion: The End of the Healing Journey 217
    It's Time to Come Home

Epilogue: Quarried Deep 225

Acknowledgments: Lifted Up 229

Notes..233

He heals the brokenhearted
and
binds up their wounds.
Psalm 147:3

Drawn from a Well

In an era when most communicators spare no opinion and share every impulsive thought, Anne Graham Lotz measures her speech and thinks before she writes. So by the time I picked up a book entitled *Wounded by God's People* with her name on it, I was already sitting up straighter, ears perked, ready to hear what she had to say. I knew two things before I started: Anne was utterly convinced of the leading of God to write it, and her own hurt had gone deep enough to sustain the holy passion to finish it. Authors don't always choose their books. Their path, and more often their pain, do the picking.

Anne uses the biblical story of Hagar to show how a young Egyptian slave was wounded by one of God's people — in fact, by one whom God called His friend, Abraham. The ink that it took to write the following chapters was drawn from a well much like the one God opened Hagar's eyes to see in the book of Genesis. Anne will take you there with her just as she took me. You may also discover as I did that you've left some matters untended and that it's time for God to address them, rinse them with water from that well, and repair them. Anne draws on her own journey not to exploit, but to explore, not to villainize, but to empathize. And she invites you along on the road to a healing heart.

Wounds caused by our own people aren't the same as the wounds of an enemy. We can't chalk them up to random acts of unkindness. They're personal. They are inflicted by people who know us, by people we believed have loved us or at least thought kindly of us. When it is not just *our* people but *God's* people, the wound can gape wide open into a maelstrom of confusion.

Alienation.

Isolation.

Shame.

In the words of James, "These things should not be so, my brothers and sisters" (James 3:10b, NET). But unfortunately they are. And they are probably to be expected in this unfinished world among unfinished people like you and me.

Praise God, we are not without remedy. Nor are we without fellowship. The Bible records a great cloud of witnesses who have been injured within their own community and put outside the camp in one way or another. As New Testament believers, we will find that enduring this brand of pain is a profoundly impactful way we fellowship in the suffering of Christ. For Him to have been tried and tempted and torn in all ways such as we have — yet without sin — His betrayer, Judas, had to come from His own close circle. Betrayal betrays a certain camaraderie. A relationship had existed that was then found dispensable.

With the character we are blessed to expect from Anne, she speaks in these pages not only about being wounded, but also about how easily we can wound. I've been that person. You may have been too. Thankfully, wounders can also find healing and wholeness. We're all within God's reach. We're all addressed in His Word, included in His wise counsel, and thoroughly immersed in His unfathomable love. He is a well that will never run dry.

I am so thankful for Anne Graham Lotz. She is a grace gift to the Body of Christ. A rarity, I believe, in our culture. God alone knows what He has called her to endure for purposes well beyond her own sake and sanctification. I am convinced that much of what she shares with such transparency and humility in these pages was appointed to her path because God knew she wouldn't keep her healing to herself. That's the nature of the gospel. When you find good news at a bad time, you have to tell it.

Crack open these pages and you'll find a God who has already found you right there in that wilderness. Oh, may He speak so tenderly to you.

Beth Moore
Living Proof Ministries

Jesus Understands

He Was Wounded Too

As I look back on my life, it saddens me to acknowledge that some of my most painful wounds were inflicted by religious people — God's people. Those who have been the most hurtful, those who have been the most unkind, those who have betrayed, slandered, and undermined me have been those who have also called themselves by God's name. They have been considered Christians by themselves and by others. Yet they have been men and women whose words and behavior are inconsistent with what they say they believe and contradict what God says. Even now, I shake my head in near disbelief as I recall some of the painful experiences I will share with you in this book.

A complicating factor for those of us who have been wounded by the behavior of Christians such as these is that we often suffer in silence. Which makes me wonder ... are you one of us? Are you like the dear woman who suffered in silence and expressed her wounding in a letter to me:

I can't tell you how many times I have cried deep tears that shook my whole body because of painful things that happened to me in my church.... I was so hurt I stopped attending church for a good while.... I have recently returned to a new church, but I have often wondered what I did wrong or how I could have handled the past situation better. I think the rumor at my old church is that I left the church because I was depressed or something ... primarily because I kept quiet rather than attempting to defend my position. I didn't want anything I said to enter the gossip mill and hurt those who had hurt me.

I have decided to break the silence. As I reflect on the wounds that have been inflicted intentionally and unintentionally on me and on others, I feel it's time to say something. It's time to put this on the table and call out the "sin that's in the camp."[1]

As painful and devastating as wounds inflicted by God's people can be, they have made me more determined to live out what I believe authentically. I am deeply motivated to know God. I want to know Him as He truly is, not through the distorted reflection of those who called themselves by His name. And I want to make Him known to others as accurately, winsomely, clearly, and compellingly as I can.

While I don't know God as well as I want to, or as well as I should, I do know Him well enough to know that Jesus understands, because He was wounded too. It was part of God's divine plan of redemption for Jesus to be wounded and rejected by those He came to save: "He came to his own, and those who were His own did not receive Him."[2] The very people who knew the messianic prophecies better than anyone else, the very ones who should have been first in line to recognize and worship Him, the religious, educated, knowledgeable leaders of God's people, were the very ones who rejected Jesus. The very ones who called themselves the children of God stubbornly hardened their hearts against His Son. Yes, the Son of God understands what it feels like to be wounded by cruel rejection. The religious people of His day aimed their verbal missiles at Him, then took decisive action against Him ...

"Some of the teachers of the law said to themselves, 'This fellow is blaspheming!' "[3]

"The Pharisees said, 'It is by the prince of demons that he drives out demons.' "[4]

"The Pharisees went out and plotted how they might kill Jesus."[5]

"Then the Pharisees went out and laid plans to trap him in his words."[6]

"Then the chief priests and the elders of the people ... plotted to arrest Jesus in some sly way and kill him."[7]

"Those who had arrested Jesus ... spit in his face and struck him with their fists. Others slapped him."[8]

"All the chief priests and the elders of the people came to the decision to put Jesus to death. They bound him, led him away and handed him over to Pilate, the governor.... He had Jesus flogged, and handed him over to be crucified."[9]

The words coming at Him from very powerful, very religious men must have felt like repeated punches to the gut. Can you feel His pain? Peter did. He was an eyewitness to the assaults on Jesus. But Peter also learned from them. Here is how he described what He saw in Jesus: "When they hurled their insults at him, he did not retaliate; when he suffered, he made no threats. Instead, he entrusted himself to him who judges justly."[10]

If ever someone had the right to protest, *This isn't right, this isn't fair, I don't deserve this*, it was Jesus.

If ever someone had the right to walk out and walk away, it was Jesus.

If ever someone had an excuse to complain, feel sorry for
    Himself, find fault with God, it was Jesus.
If ever someone had the right to retaliate and — literally —
    condemn those who mistreated Him, it was Jesus.

Instead, Jesus entrusted Himself to God. He knew His beloved
Father well enough to know that these very religious people,
although they considered themselves God's representatives on earth,
were nothing of the sort. They were wicked, sinful pretenders who
would one day stand before God and give an account for what they
had done.

It never ceases to amaze me that the most vicious lies, the most
violent attacks, the ultimate rejection of Jesus, came not from the
Romans or the Greeks or the pagans or the secularists, but from Israelites who were considered by themselves and others the children of
God. God's people.

So I refuse to let religious phonies destroy my heart for the One
who loves me and draws close to me when I am wounded. I refuse
to be robbed of life's greatest treasure — a personal, permanent, passionate relationship with God through faith in Jesus.

Dear wounded believer-in-exile, what is your story? What chapter
is being written today? Is your spirit lying in the dust of your wilderness wandering? Can you hear His voice calling to you? Don't reject
the God of those who rejected you. Rejecting God doesn't hurt them;
it only hurts you. You are the one who has been devastated. And you
are the one God is calling.

Run to God and cling to Him. God understands every verbal barb,
every covert injustice, every emotional shard, every leering look,
every jeering smirk. But He also keeps the books, and one day He
will make everything right.

In the meantime, "Let us fix our eyes on Jesus, the author and per-fecter of our faith, who for the joy set before him endured the cross, scorning its shame, and sat down at the right hand of the throne of God. Consider him who endured such opposition from sinful men, so that you will not grow weary and lose heart."[11] *Jesus understands!* Because He was wounded too.

Healing Is a Journey

You Are Invited to Begin

Almost everyone I know has been wounded to one degree or another. It doesn't matter if a person is young or old, rich or poor, intelligent or ignorant, healthy or infirm, educated or illiterate. We've all experienced wounds. While some are superficial and others are destructively deep, all wounds hurt. If left to their natural course, they can fester into deep bitterness, resentment, and anger that infects other seemingly unrelated aspects of our lives. Maybe that's one reason the Bible has so much to say about wounds. And the wounded. And the wounders. Throughout Scripture, we feel the pain, we hear the cries, we see the revenge. Often we observe the wounded becoming wounders with the cycle being repeated from person to person and generation to generation. But throughout the gripping narratives, God's love is contrasted with the pain like sunlight emerging in silver streaks from behind a blackened cloud. Because God's love not only comforts and redeems, it heals.

One such narrative is the story I am about to unfold for you in this book. It's a small story that is a footnote to a greater one, like a smaller tributary to a bigger river.

The Mississippi is a mighty river. It is the greatest river system in North America and one of the longest, largest rivers in the world. It is so powerful that two of its tributaries are major rivers in themselves, the Ohio River and the Missouri River.

The "tributary," or smaller story, was placed on my heart when I wrote *The Magnificent Obsession*,[1] which chronicles Abraham's journey of faith.[2] His extraordinary life is a mighty river that runs through human history, significantly impacting our world for four thousand years.

Tucked into Abraham's biography is a tributary story that becomes in itself a significant river in the flow of human history. It is the story of Hagar, a young Egyptian slave with whom Abraham had a son named Ishmael — a man to whom many contemporary Arab peoples trace their lineage, and the one from whom all Muslims believe they have descended.

While I was immersed in studying Abraham's story, Hagar caught my attention. She stood out because she was wounded — not physically, but in ways that were as emotionally and spiritually painful as any injury to a body would be. Some wounds were provoked by her own bad behavior, but others were inflicted by those who were considered to be God's people.

I too have been wounded by God's people. Some wounds have been deeper than others, some seemed to have come out of nowhere, some have been provoked by my own bad behavior, yet all of the wounds have been deeply painful. And they seemed to hurt even more when the wounders wrapped their behavior in a semblance of religion or piety.

God has used the story of Hagar to shine the light of His truth into my own heart, revealing that not only have I been wounded, but that

I have been a wounder. The resulting guilt and grief have increased my burden to write this book, because I have discovered that God can truly redeem the pain, the guilt, and the grief. I want to share His love with you, inviting you to embark on a healing journey.

And it is a journey. There is no quick fix. But there are specific steps to take that will lead you out of the miry pit your wounds have dug — a pit where bitterness is rooted and joy is robbed and relationships are shattered.

The first step of the journey is to acknowledge your pain. Stop covering it up, rationalizing it, defending it, excusing it, ignoring it. Just admit it. Now. Once you've taken the initial step, I'll lead you ever so gently along the path of discovery Hagar has marked out for us.

So ...

If you are among those who have been so deeply hurt that you have confused God's imperfect people with God and perhaps have even run away from Him as a result;

If you are one who is guilty of wounding and offending others in God's name, only to find yourself wounded as a result, robbed of your own peace and joy;

If you are caught up in a generational cycle of pain that has convinced you there is no way out ...

Whatever your hurts may be, my prayer is that the following pages will ...

raise you up out of the pit into a fresh encounter with God.

lead you to reclaim the joy and peace of God's presence.

remove the sting and searing pain as God's blessings begin to flow.

enlarge your vision of God's purpose for your life that is greater than you thought.

My prayer is that, along with Hagar, you will discover the redemptive power of God's love and be healed of your hurts. Because God loves the wounded. And the wounders. I know . . .

I identify in varying degrees not only with Hagar, but with each character in her story, including the story-within-the-story that is woven throughout the shadows of her life. It's a beautiful and tender love story — not about her relationship with Abraham, but about her relationship with God. God engages in an intentional, passionate pursuit of an Egyptian slave who ultimately becomes the mother of nations. As you read, I pray the God of Hagar opens your eyes, and your heart, to Him . . . and to His pursuit of you.

Anne Graham Lotz

The Biblical Story
of Hagar

When Abram came to Egypt, the Egyptians ... treated Abram well ... and Abram acquired sheep and cattle, male and female donkeys, menservants and maidservants, and camels....

So Abram went up from Egypt to the Negev, with his wife and everything he had....

Now Sarai, Abram's wife, had borne him no children. But she had an Egyptian maidservant named Hagar; so she said to Abram, "The LORD has kept me from having children. Go, sleep with my maidservant; perhaps I can build a family through her."

Abram agreed to what Sarai said. So after Abram had been living in Canaan ten years, Sarai his wife took her Egyptian maidservant Hagar and gave her to her husband to be his wife. He slept with Hagar, and she conceived.

When she knew she was pregnant, she began to despise her mistress. Then Sarai said to Abram, "You are responsible for the wrong I am suffering. I put my servant in your arms, and now that she knows she is pregnant, she despises me. May the LORD judge between you and me."

"Your servant is in your hands," Abram said. "Do with her whatever you think best." Then Sarai mistreated Hagar; so she fled from her.

The angel of the LORD found Hagar near a spring in the desert; it was the spring that is beside the road to Shur. And he said, "Hagar, servant of Sarai, where have you come from, and where are you going?"

"I'm running away from my mistress Sarai," she answered.

Then the angel of the LORD told her, "Go back to your mistress and submit to her." The angel added, "I will so increase your descendants that they will be too numerous to count."

The angel of the LORD also said to her:

> "You are now with child
>   and you will have a son.
> You shall name him Ishmael,[1]
>   for the LORD has heard of your misery.
> He will be a wild donkey of a man;
>   his hand will be against everyone
>   and everyone's hand against him,
> and he will live in hostility
>   toward all his brothers."

She gave this name to the LORD who spoke to her: "You are the God who sees me," for she said, "I have now seen the One who sees me." That is why the well was called Beer Lahai Roi; it is still there, between Kadesh and Bered.

So Hagar bore Abram a son, and Abram gave the name Ishmael to the son she had borne. Abram was eighty-six years old when Hagar bore him Ishmael. . . .

Now the LORD was gracious to Sarah as He had said, and the LORD did for Sarah what He had promised. Sarah became pregnant and bore a son to Abraham in his old age, at the very time God had promised him. Abraham gave the name Isaac to the son Sarah bore him. When his son Isaac was eight days old, Abraham circumcised him, as God commanded him. Abraham was a hundred years old when his son Isaac was born to him.

Sarah said, "God has brought me laughter, and everyone who hears about this will laugh with me." And she added, "Who would have said to Abraham that Sarah would nurse children? Yet I have borne him a son in his old age."

The child grew and was weaned, and on the day Isaac was weaned Abraham held a great feast. But Sarah saw that the son whom Hagar the Egyptian had borne to Abraham was mocking, and she said to Abraham, "Get rid of that slave woman and her son, for that slave woman's son will never share in the inheritance with my son Isaac."

The matter distressed Abraham greatly because it concerned his son. But God said to him, "Do not be so distressed about the boy and your maidservant. Listen to whatever Sarah tells you, because it is through Isaac that your offspring will be reckoned. I will make the son of the maidservant into a nation also, because he is your offspring."

Early the next morning Abraham took some food and a skin of water and gave them to Hagar. He set them on her shoulders and then sent her off with the boy. She went on her way and wandered in the desert of Beersheba.

When the water in the skin was gone, she put the boy under one of the bushes. Then she went off and sat down nearby, about a bowshot away, for she thought, "I cannot watch the boy die." And as she sat there nearby, she began to sob.

God heard the boy crying, and the angel of God called to Hagar from heaven and said to her, "What is the matter, Hagar? Do not be afraid; God has heard the boy crying as he lies there. Lift the boy up and take him by the hand, for I will make him into a great nation."

Then God opened her eyes and she saw a well of water. So she went and filled the skin with water and gave the boy a drink.

God was with the boy as he grew up. He lived in the desert and became an archer. While he was living in the Desert of Paran, his mother got a wife for him from Egypt.[2]

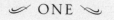

ONE

Loved by God
on the Periphery

*God Is Not
an Elitist*

Now there was a famine in the land, and Abram went down to Egypt to live there for a while because the famine was severe. As he was about to enter Egypt, he said to his wife Sarai, "I know what a beautiful woman you are. When the Egyptians see you, they will say, 'This is his wife.' Then they will kill me but will let you live. Say you are my sister, so that I will be treated well for your sake and my life will be spared because of you."

When Abram came to Egypt, the Egyptians saw that she was a very beautiful woman. And when Pharaoh's officials saw her, they praised her to Pharaoh, and she was taken into his palace. He treated Abram well for her sake, and Abram acquired sheep and cattle, male and female donkeys, menservants and maidservants, and camels.

But the LORD inflicted serious diseases on Pharaoh and his household because of Abram's wife Sarai. So Pharaoh summoned Abram. "What have you done to me?" he said. "Why didn't you tell me she was your wife? Why did you say, 'She is my sister,' so that I took her to be my wife? Now then, here is your wife. Take her and go!" Then Pharaoh gave orders about Abram to his men, and they sent him on his way, with his wife and everything he had. . . .

So Abram went up from Egypt to the Negev, with his wife and everything he had . . .

Genesis 12:10–20; 13:1

All of us know what it feels like to be on the periphery. My husband and I suddenly found ourselves on the "outside" after we had been profoundly rejected by our church. Though it happened many years ago, the painful memory still lingers.

The memory resurfaced when I was recently stopped at the traffic light in front of our former church. As I gazed at the beautiful, columned brick structure, with the spire pointing towards the cobalt blue sky above, I seemed to hear once again the faint echoes of applause in the sanctuary. It had been filled with people as my husband, Danny, was voted out of a strategic leadership position. His previous years of faithful service to the church — as chairman of the board of deacons, chairman of the men's fellowship, and an adult Sunday school teacher — no longer seemed to matter. On that Sunday morning, during what was described as a "worship service," our ears rang with the sound of rejection.

The congregation applauded as the vote was announced. Six hundred members against Danny to two hundred for him. The lopsided results left no room for doubt or discussion as to the desire of the church body. They wanted Danny out. Following the service, the five-minute walk to the parking lot seemed more like a five-mile trek through the wilderness. With my eyes blurred and my mind reeling from what we had just experienced, I held Danny's hand as we numbly walked to the car. Bottom line, our impeachable offense was that we believed, lived by, and taught the Bible as the inerrant, inspired, authoritative Word of God. We were innocent casualties caught up in the political power struggles of a denomination that at the time was battling over this very issue.

We dearly loved the people in that church. We had served them faithfully and sacrificially for more than fifteen years. Our children had been born and baptized there. I will tell you very candidly that being rejected by that church *hurt*. And it hurts to this day. We were wounded.

Have you been wounded by God's people too? Have you been made to feel that you were on the outside of God's inner circle? Sometimes we agree with that rejection because we don't think we are good enough for God, lovable enough for God, worthy enough to be on the inside anyway. Such thinking can be the result of having been mistreated in some way by those who call themselves by His name. Or the treatment confirms what we had thought anyway. Rejection, disapproval, or abuse by God's people can be devastating because if you and I are not careful, we may confuse God's people with God. And God's people don't always act like God's people should.

The way you and I handle being rejected and wounded is critical. Our response can lead to healing ... or to even more hurt.

I fully understand if you have been so hurt by God's people that you have made the choice to walk away — not just from the church, not just from Christians, not just from those who call themselves by God's name, but from God. I could have too. Instead, God found me — and loved me — on the periphery. Why? Because God is not an elitist. He associates not only with those who appear to be part of an inner circle, but with those who have been made to feel they are on the outside.

The Bible is full of stories about how God's love is broad enough, deep enough, high enough, and long enough to draw in those who are treated as outsiders. Hagar's story is a poignant one.

Hagar was one of the many young Egyptian women who served in Pharaoh's palace. The Bible doesn't tell us if she was born into slavery or if she had been forced into it for the payment of a debt or for some other reason. History gives us no details, but it's safe to assume her life was not her own. She was a slave who lived at the whim of Pharaoh. It takes no imagination to assume that her status surely resulted in multiple wounds of one form or another.

One day, Pharaoh took a dazzlingly beautiful new wife. The entire palace buzzed with news about the exotic "princess" from a faraway land who had entered Egypt with her brother. The princess, Sarah, had been quickly scooped up by government officials as a sparkling addition to the king's collection of wives.[1]

The king had been so enthralled by his new wife that he had showered her brother, Abraham, with gifts: "For her sake,... Abram acquired sheep and cattle, male and female donkeys, menservants and maidservants, and camels."[2] And that's where Hagar's life took a dramatic turn, through no choice of her own. She was plucked out of obscurity and placed onto the world stage of human history because she was one of the gifts Pharaoh gave in gratitude to Abraham.

But things were not as they seemed. Abraham wasn't just Sarah's half-brother; he was also her husband.[3] And he had such a unique relationship with the living God that the way people treated Abraham and his family, God considered treatment of Himself.[4] So when Sarah was placed into a dangerous, compromising position, vulnerable to being defiled by a pagan king, God intervened. To protect Sarah physically, as well as to guard her reputation, He struck everyone in the palace with serious diseases.[5]

Pharaoh connected the dots between the diseases, his new wife, her brother, and an angry God. The result was that Abraham's deception was exposed. He was publicly rebuked by Pharaoh, then thrown out of Egypt along with Sarah and everything he had, which included Hagar.[6]

Hagar suddenly found herself uprooted from all she had ever known. She went from living in a luxurious palace — even if she had resided in the servants' quarters — to living in animal-skin tents with a nomadic people whose language she didn't understand, whose food was strange, whose clothes were relatively plain, and whose ways were foreign to her. Her status is possibly revealed by her placement in the list of gifts given to Abraham — below the sheep, cattle, and donkeys, and just above the camels. She seemed to be nothing more than the possession of a foreigner. Hagar was an outsider ... an outsider to her familiar Egyptian culture now that she belonged to Abraham and Sarah, but also an outsider to Abraham's household since she was an Egyptian. She was doubly outside, belonging nowhere.

Have you ever felt that you just didn't belong anywhere? Maybe you've been displaced because of a natural disaster, or a divorce, or eviction from your home, or termination from your job. If you married into a different race, or nationality, or culture, or language, or economic strata, or educational level, you may suddenly have discovered you are now living your life on the periphery of your family or friends ... or your spouse's family and friends. As awkward and uncomfortable and lonely as that may be — as stunning as it can be to have your private world turned upside down in the blink of an eye — I'm not sure it's the same pain as that of finding yourself on the outside of the church because you've been driven there by

God's people who have rejected you. Somehow, factoring God into the equation makes the rejection hurt worse.

As we continue our journey with Hagar, we will discover that her wounds increased to include those inflicted by God's people. In her pain, she behaved badly and became a wounder. As a result, she was wounded even more deeply, caught up in a cycle of pain that enveloped those around her, including her own son. And so she ran to the far limits of the outside — she ran to the periphery.

But God loved Hagar. He loves those who just can't take it anymore and who run away. In fact, the Bible is filled with stories of His love for those like Hagar. One such story is that of Rahab.

Rahab was a Canaanite prostitute. As such, she too was doubly outside. As a prostitute she lived life on the periphery of acceptable behavior, and as a Canaanite, she was outside of God's people, the children of Israel. She was a very unlikely candidate for God's attention, much less His redeeming love.

Her story is found in the Old Testament book of Joshua.[7] And it doesn't take much imagination to conclude that Rahab had been used and abused by others. In fact, her culture glamorized abuse, idolized immorality, and literally worshiped wickedness and evil. Human sacrifice and sex orgies were part of their religious expression. No thought was given to the feelings of victims or the consequences of indulging in animalistic desires.

Rahab was undoubtedly trapped in a life she did not want. She couldn't go back — there was no way to untangle years of sin and trauma in an effort to take up the life she had before she was a prostitute. She couldn't go forward because her future held no hope. Who would care enough to help a prostitute? And besides, everyone in her life was a Canaanite. She knew of no one who thought differently, lived differently, or felt differently. All she could do was survive one day at a time, trying to stifle the pain from wounds both old and new. She was trapped in a life of sexual degradation and humiliation. Inside, she must have been filled with silent screams to any god who was out there who was real and could save her.

Little did Rahab know that there was, indeed, a God who was real and who had heard her inaudible cries. In the omniscient sovereignty of God, Rahab's longing for salvation and freedom coincided with a momentous occasion in divine history. After forty years of wandering, the entire nation of Israel, numbering several million people, was at last poised to enter the Promised Land. Soon, the Israelites would possess the land God had promised to Abraham, Isaac, and Jacob. The only thing blocking their progress was Jericho, a seemingly impregnable enemy fortress and the city in which Rahab lived.

The residents within Jericho's fortified walls had heard of the God of Israel — how He had decimated Egypt with a series of plagues and then destroyed the world-class Egyptian army in an unparalleled act of supernatural power. And they knew about other miracles as well: How God had led them through the wilderness for forty years with a cloud to protect them from the heat of the day and a fiery pillar to provide light and heat during the night; how He had quenched their thirst by giving them water from a rock; how He had fed them every morning with bread that appeared on the ground and every evening with quail that flew into their encampment; how He had given the Israelites victory over enemies who tried to thwart their progress. Oh, yes! The Canaanites living in Jericho, including Rahab, had heard of the God of Israel.[8] So when they awoke one morning to find that they were in Israel's crosshairs, their hearts melted and everyone's courage failed.[9] Their fear must have then intensified into near paralysis when instead of immediately attacking, the Israelites simply set up camp outside the city walls and waited ... *for what?*

The Bible tells us that Joshua, the commander of the Israelites, used that waiting time to send spies into Jericho. He must have wanted answers to a whole host of logistical questions: *Is there more than one wall? How thick are the walls? How many gates are there in the walls? How many armed men are prepared to defend the city?* But as the story unfolds, we know that the military assessment proved unnecessary. God had an entirely different idea about how to bring down the enemy fortress — and it had nothing to do with military strategy, the number of enemy soldiers, the access or the egress.

Could it be that God put the entire Israelite advance on hold because He had heard the cry of one person? A Canaanite, not an Israelite? The cry of a woman, not a man? The cry of a prostitute, not a noble woman? Though she lived on the periphery of God's people and was unquestionably an outsider, Rahab nevertheless had eyes to see, ears to hear, a heart to hope, and a will to throw herself on God's mercy. Could it be that God, in answer to Rahab's cry, postponed Israel's advance into the Promised Land for several days in order to save *just one person*?

When Israel's spies surfaced in Rahab's brothel seeking information, it became obvious that she had been on a spiritual quest and arrived at an inescapable conclusion: *Israel's God is the one true God.*[10] So she boldly put out a very small tendril of faith, wrapping it around the character of the God about whom she had heard. Summoning her courage and knowing this was her only chance for deliverance, she seized the opportunity to make a deal with the spies: she would spare their lives if they would save hers. Her desire was to belong to the God of Israel. I wonder if she held her breath as she waited for their answer. If so, she didn't have to hold it for long. They agreed! Their words were surely heaven's answer to her heart's cry. If she would hide them and then help them escape the city, they would see to it that she and all in her house were saved when Jericho was destroyed.

Approximately three weeks later, the Israelites broke camp and advanced. When the walls of Jericho fell in a terrifying mushroom cloud of dust and debris, only one section remained standing. Perched on the top of that section was Rahab's house, marked by a scarlet cord dangling from her window to identify her location to the invading Israelite army. She had kept her part of the deal. As she gazed out at the destruction from her precarious position, she must have had a moment of sheer panic. Would the spies keep their part of the deal? Would their God really care about one Canaanite prostitute?

I can only imagine Rahab's terror as she felt the earthquake-like tremor when the walls collapsed and she was surrounded by all the terrifying sounds of battle — clashing weapons and the cries of those in the city being put to death, the rebel-like yell of Israelite soldiers as they advanced on the now exposed city, and then the sound of soldiers' feet pounding up her steps. Her door must have suddenly burst open, and Israelites covered with dust shouted, "Rahab, you're saved! The God of Israel has commanded us to save you and all that are in your house!"[11] Then Rahab knew for certain — *God is real!* And merciful! And He truly does love those who are on the periphery.

Like Rahab, I wonder if you've been considered an outsider ... on the periphery ... for a long time. Perhaps generations of your family have lived separated from the one living God — separated from truth, real goodness, righteousness, and holiness. Wounding can actually be a byproduct of our culture's creed ...

Don't get mad, get even.

Don't let anyone walk over you.

Insist on your rights.

Assert yourself.

Whatever feels right is right.

If it works, do it.

Successful people don't fail.

More money means more happiness.

Tell people what they want to hear; never mind the truth.

Grab all the gusto you can.

If you don't put your interests first, who will?

Because you've been raised in this culture, have these misguided values trapped you in a fortress-like environment that is suffocating your spirit? Like Rahab, do you feel you are hopelessly stuck behind walls and walls of sin that impact ...

your memories and your marriage,

your children and your career,

your lifestyle and your outlook,

your culture and your choices,

your environment and your entertainment,

your attitude and your ambition,

your reactions and your reasoning ...

Sin that's like a powerful Canaanite fortress from which you can't escape? Sin that has separated you from God and placed you on the outside.

As you read this, if your own heart has been quickened with longing for a different way of life, a longing to be set free, for true salvation from sin, then I invite you to cry out to the God of Rahab. He is the same today as He was in her day. He has ears to hear the heartfelt cry of one person, no matter who you are or where you are or how long you have been there. Use the words of the following prayer if you need help articulating your cry.

Dear God,

I'm living in my own version of Jericho — I feel trapped in a life and culture of sinful thoughts, actions, and patterns. My spirit is suffocating. I've been wounded so deeply and so continuously that I don't know what it's like to live without feeling pain every moment of every day. Please save me. Deliver me. I'm so very tired of hurting.

I confess that some of my wounds are self-inflicted. Others have come as the consequence of how I have wounded others. I'm a sinner — it's who I am and what I do.[12] I sin. And I know I'm separated from You. I'm trapped behind thick walls that have been built up over weeks, months, years, decades, generations, and these walls are barriers between You and me.

Please break down the walls and forgive me of my sin. Save me. Deliver me. Set me free. I want to be Yours.

I believe Jesus is Your Son. You sent Him into my Jericho to make a way for me to be saved. I believe He died to set me free. Right now, would You forgive me of all of my sin for His sake?[13] I believe that Jesus rose from the dead to give me life. Please give me the freedom of eternal life, which I know will be a heavenly home when I die.[14] But I also know that it's a personal relationship with You right now.[15]

I choose to leave Jericho and my old way of living. I invite You to come into my life.[16] Like the Israelites of old, I will follow You wherever You lead.[17]

Amen.

Listen quietly with the ears of your heart. Can you hear the sound of His feet rushing up the stairs into your life ... *You're saved! The God of Rahab has commanded Me to save you.[18]*

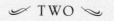

TWO

Life Is Hard

*Everyone
Is Wounded*

Abram had become very wealthy in livestock and in silver and gold.

From the Negev he went from place to place until he came to Bethel, to the place between Bethel and Ai where his tent had been earlier and where he had first built an altar. There Abram called on the name of the LORD.

Now Lot, who was moving about with Abram, also had flocks and herds and tents. But the land could not support them while they stayed together, for their possessions were so great that they were not able to stay together. And quarreling arose between Abram's herdsmen and the herdsmen of Lot. The Canaanites and Perizzites were also living in the land at that time.

So Abram said to Lot, "Let's not have any quarreling between you and me, or between your herdsmen and mine, for we are brothers. Is not the whole land before you? Let's part company. If you go to the left, I'll go to the right; if you go to the right, I'll go to the left."

Lot looked up and saw that the whole plain of the Jordan was well watered, like the garden of the LORD, like the land of Egypt, toward Zoar. (This was before the LORD destroyed Sodom and Gomorrah.) So Lot chose for himself the whole plain of the Jordan and set out toward the east. The two men parted company. . . .

The LORD said to Abram after Lot had parted from him, "Lift up your eyes from where you are and look north and south, east and west. All the land that you see I will give to you and your offspring forever. I will make your offspring like the dust of the earth, so that if anyone could count the dust, then your offspring could be counted. Go, walk through the length and breadth of the land, for I am giving it to you."

So Abram moved his tents and went to live near the great trees of Mamre at Hebron, where he built an altar to the LORD.

Genesis 13:2 - 11, 14 - 18

When do wounds begin? Who can remember the first one? And who can claim a life without them?

Among my earliest memories of being wounded is an experience I had in grade school. My fifth-grade teacher was a retired Presbyterian missionary. She was what my younger sister and I described at the time as an "old maid." She looked like she came from central casting — gray hair pulled back in a tight bun, granite-like face seamed with wrinkles and carved into a disapproving frown, mouth tightened in a constant grimace, sharp eyes that missed nothing — and she did not like me. Her stern demeanor, our dark classroom, and lessons that seemed to drag on forever were a deadly combination for an energetic child. So from time to time, a deep and spontaneous sigh escaped from my lips. She glaringly told me one afternoon in no uncertain terms that if I sighed one more time in class, she would slap my face! I took a deep breath, let it out slowly, and, believe you me, silently. My mother never understood why it was so hard for me to view missionaries as she did, as the aristocracy of heaven. If that were actually true, I surmised, I'd be very happy to remain a peasant.

As I remember my own childhood, it's sobering to contemplate the impact that a stern, unattractive, unloving, unkind adult can have on a child. Especially if that person is also considered to be a mature Christian. Had my fifth-grade teacher's demeanor and actions not been more than offset by my own deeply spiritual mother, whose beauty, wit, grace, and compassion were so charming, I'm sure I would never have had such a strong desire to be a mature Christian myself.

But the first time I remember being more seriously wounded by those who called themselves Christians was in ninth grade. My parents had sent me off to a Christian boarding school where my older sister was also in attendance. While my sister was practically a poster child for the school, seated at the head table during meal times and introduced to any and every visiting dignitary, I was shuffled to the periphery. I was criticized and yelled at for no reason that I was aware of. When I developed a close friendship with another student as a buffer to the mistreatment, the headmistress actually accused me of having homosexual tendencies. I didn't even know what a homosexual was. I remember looking up the word in the dictionary and still not comprehending what it meant or how it could possibly apply to me. But one thing was clear. I was definitely on the outside of any inner circle. Within three months, I had been reprimanded for talking back to the headmistress, made something of a reputation for myself as a rebel, and landed in the infirmary with a persistent illness. And I learned the hard way that wounds inflicted on us, even if they are only wounds resulting from the laceration of words, can make us physically ill. My mother removed me from the school for several months so I could recover at home, but then sent me back to finish out the year. At the end of that first school year, I was transferred from the boarding school to the public high school in our mountain county in Western North Carolina, where I thrived.

A couple of years later, I became interested in fashion modeling, and my mother helped arrange some low-key but fun jobs for me in nearby Asheville. As a result, I began wearing makeup, bleached my hair, and one Sunday morning had the audacity to wear a man's hat, such as I had seen on a *Vogue* model, to the little Presbyterian church we were members of in Montreal. I can still remember sitting in the fourth row of the church with my mother and siblings, waiting for the service to begin. I watched as a distinguished elderly lady rose from her seat, walked stiffly over to my mother, and with a stern look pronounced judgment on me — and on my mother for allowing me to wear a man's hat, especially to church. "And, by the way," she added, "I've been meaning to speak to you, Ruth, about the way you've allowed Anne to bleach her hair and wear makeup like that." My mother smiled, thanked the lady for her advice, then winked at me and told me I looked beautiful. Unique, but beautiful.

This seemingly small wound that took place in church was the first of a series of others that I endure to this day. Wounds inflicted when those within the church have pronounced judgment on me, not for the way I look, but for the way I speak … and where I speak … and to whom I speak.

These are just a few of my earliest experiences of feeling hurt and alienated by God's people. They may seem mild all these years later, but I remember them keenly because of how much they hurt at the time — and because they were the first of many such experiences to come. I will share more stories as the book unfolds. But through all of these painful situations, God, in His infinite grace, helped me to distinguish between His people and Himself. With each hurtful experience, I was confronted with a choice: *Would I reject Him because I was rejected by them?* Rather than rehash the decision every time I was rejected, I decided years ago that once and for all I was committed to live my life for God, regardless of the way He was represented by others. In other words, other people's treatment of me would in no way affect my relationship with Him, unless it was to drive me closer to Him … to strengthen my faith in Him … to intensify my pursuit of knowing Him as He is and not for the tarnished image of Him that His people sometimes reflect. It was a decision that has proven valuable. Because as protected and prayed for as my family is and has been, without going into detail I can tell you that there have been wounds on top of wounds. Betrayal, adultery, rape, drunkenness, theft, drug addiction, lying, and other acts of the sinful nature have manifested themselves in my extended family.[1] Actions motivated by jealousy, ambition, pride, lust, and greed — just plain old sin — have resulted in wounds that have inflicted untold damage on the wounded. Does that surprise you? That a preacher's extended family not only includes deeply wounded people, but also includes wounders? Yet it does. Which is one reason I know that God's love heals. He can redeem the wounded. And forgive the wounders.

When we think about it, why should my family be exempt from wounds anyway? The Bible says that all have sinned — that the heart of man is desperately wicked — and we live in a fallen world.[2] I dare to say that all families carry wounds inflicted by each other to a greater or lesser degree. Family life can be hard.

And "family" life was increasingly hard for Hagar. As a slave, wounds were woven into the very fabric of her existence. When she left Egypt, as devastating as this could have been for a young girl, I wonder if she may at first actually have viewed it as an adventure! She may have been filled with excitement as she anticipated exploring beyond the palace walls and Egypt's borders. She may have been thrilled to escape the authority of the palace officials and Pharaoh himself, and eager to serve Sarah, the breathtakingly beautiful princess. Perhaps to Hagar this seemed like the great escape from her wounded life that she had dreamt of but never thought she would actually experience.

Reflecting back on the early years of our lives, I expect most of us tended to view the world with bright, eager eyes. We were filled with the anticipation of adventure and discovery. The possibilities seemed limitless to our young imaginations and dreams. But then reality set in.

When did real life hit you? Our dreams can die when we find ourselves, like Hagar, with the odds stacked against us — perhaps because of a dysfunctional family, an absentee parent, a sibling who tormented us one minute and hugged us the next, abuse by a friend or extended family member. Maybe as you grew up, you were wounded by ...

Having to work long hours at a young age to help the family make ends meet, and so were denied a more innocent childhood;

The bitterness of your parents' ugly divorce just when you needed them the most;

The unexpected death of a parent or sibling that left you feeling abandoned ... permanently;

Relocating from place to place as a parent kept looking for a better position, or traveled to another military base;

Embarking on the adventure of a new career that turned out to be very different than what you had anticipated. And very unpleasant.

Did your big break turn into a big bust? Sometimes a great escape from a wounded past can turn into something worse as we discover the wounds were not just from without, but they were within. So regardless of where we go, what we do, who we are with, we carry those wounds with us.

Life can be hard, can't it? From the moment we leave the comfort of our mother's womb and the doctor or midwife slaps our little bottoms to make us cry our first deep breath, we are hurt. Everyone who lives longer than a day experiences a variety of hurts. Life hurts! Because life *is* hard.

Hagar's life with Abraham and Sarah may not have been hard initially. She appears to have lived comfortably and happily in Abraham's household for about ten years after leaving Egypt. She may have felt she had left her hard way of life behind her for good. With her youth, I expect she learned their language quickly, adapted to their nomadic lifestyle easily, and became accustomed to their ways without any difficulty. If she had not fit in well, Sarah would never have thought of recommending her to Abraham, as we will see she did in the next chapter. So while Hagar could have been homesick for Egypt and all that had been familiar, there is no indication that she was. The impression is that Hagar must have embraced her new home, her new family, her new way of life, and her new future without resentment, but with acceptance and flexibility.

I wonder what she thought the first time she observed Abraham building an altar and heard him calling on the name of his God.[3] Did she ask him or Sarah or one of the other servants for an explanation? Surely she was given the answer that Abraham was worshiping the one true living God, the Lord God Most High, Creator of heaven and earth.[4] As she cleaned up after the evening meal and attended to Sarah's needs, did her mistress explain to her how God had spoken to Abraham when he was living in Ur? That God had told Abraham if he would follow Him in a life of obedient faith, he would be blessed to be a blessing to the world.[5] Did Sarah tell Hagar that one primary aspect of God's blessing to Abraham was the promise of a "seed"? A son?[6] There was no need for Sarah to tell Hagar that she had been unable to conceive that seed and bear a child. That would have been obvious. Not just by the fact that there was no son, but by the pained, empty look on Sarah's face when she spoke of the longing ... and the promise.

Hagar's masters were surely kind and good to her, and she must have related their treatment of her to their "God." The contrast between the way they lived and the way the Canaanites around them lived must have made her take their God and their faith in Him seriously. With her Egyptian background, Hagar must have recognized the Canaanites for what they were ... obscene, pornographic, selfish and self-centered, greedy, cruel ... yet wealthy and attractive. While not as sophisticated as the Egyptians, the Canaanites were very much like the culture in which she had been raised. But Abraham's family was different.

She had witnessed firsthand the difference when fighting broke out between Abraham's servants and those of his nephew Lot.[7] Abraham immediately acted to resolve the tension, while Lot used the crisis for his own advancement, seizing the best of the prime pastureland for his flocks and herds. Lot walked out with what appeared to be everything, leaving Abraham to live in a tent under the trees. What must have amazed Hagar and provoked her grudging admiration was that rather than being bitter, Abraham seemed content. Unlike the Canaanites and the Egyptians, he did not insist on his rights, or flaunt his position, or fight to acquire more possessions, or wield his power to force others to comply with what he wanted. He seemed to let go of everything and trust that God would give him what was best in the long run. Abraham seemed to be living for something bigger ... more ... greater than the here and now. It was intriguing. Hagar must have slowly come to realize that it wasn't *something* bigger. It was *Someone*. Hagar must have increasingly come to realize that the difference in Abraham's life was his God.

As the years passed, I wonder if Hagar began to care about Abraham and his family. Did she begin to desire that their prayers would be answered? Did Abraham's confidence in God's promise spill over to Hagar so that she anticipated the day he and Sarah would have a son? Over the ten-year period she served them after leaving Egypt, she must have settled down and begun to respect them as well as to care about them and trust them.

Hagar's lengthy relationship with Abraham and Sarah must have made her wounding even more agonizing. Because while all of us experience bumps and bruises along life's journey ... injustice ... unfairness ... unkindness ... meanness ... Hagar's story is not about those kinds of hurts. Her story is about wounds that were inflicted by those with whom she once felt safe and least expected to be wounders. Wounds inflicted by those she loved, respected, and trusted. Hagar was wounded by God's people.

If you have been wounded by God's people too ... wounded by those with whom you had once felt safe and least expected to be wounders ... wounded by those who you have loved, respected, and trusted ... then you understand the pain is not something you can easily or quickly overcome. In fact, you and I can carry those wounds around with us until they begin to revolve in a cycle of pain, and we, in turn, become wounders ourselves.

THREE

The Cycle of Pain

*The Wounded
Become Wounders*

Now Sarai, Abram's wife, had borne him no children. But she had an Egyptian maidservant named Hagar; so she said to Abram, "The LORD has kept me from having children. Go, sleep with my maidservant; perhaps I can build a family through her."

Abram agreed to what Sarai said. So after Abram had been living in Canaan ten years, Sarai his wife took her Egyptian maidservant Hagar and gave her to her husband to be his wife. He slept with Hagar, and she conceived.

When she knew she was pregnant, she began to despise her mistress. Then Sarai said to Abram, "You are responsible for the wrong I am suffering. I put my servant in your arms, and now that she knows she is pregnant, she despises me. May the LORD judge between you and me."

"Your servant is in your hands," Abram said. "Do with her whatever you think best." Then Sarai mistreated Hagar . . .

Genesis 16:1 - 6

The summer I was seventeen, our beloved family pastor strongly encouraged my parents to send me to a two-week Christian leadership-training institute. It was located in the mountains of a spectacularly beautiful Western state. When they took his advice and sent me, I was eager to go. I found myself plunging into all of the workshops, electives, and main sessions. After years in a public school, I looked forward to the training and the like-minded friends I would make. Friends who also wanted to grow in their relationship with God and who had a passion to make Him known to others. As the days unfolded, I became increasingly skeptical of what I was being exposed to — not because there was anything unbiblical about it, but because of the disconnect between what the staff taught and what I observed in their behavior.

One of the sessions was led by a beautiful couple who were engaged to be married and had just spent the weekend together on the coast. The young woman's eyes sparkled as she told me about their intimate times in the beach house. Other sessions were led by those who said all the right words, yet their conversations outside formal sessions struck me as proud, self-promoting, and self-righteous. When I couldn't reconcile what the leaders taught with how they lived, I lost interest in the training. As it turned out, I wasn't the only one.

I quickly developed a group of friends who were equally disenchanted, and we began slipping away during evening lectures to have fun at a nearby resort. Because I had skipped out on some of the sessions, on the last day of the institute I was confronted by one of the young women with whom I shared a suite in the hotel where the attendees were housed. She expressed the collective disappointment of the other girls, all of whom felt I had fallen far short of their expectations for Billy Graham's daughter. She then tearfully informed me that everyone in the suite was praying for me because I was so "carnal." I wasn't sure what carnal meant, but if it was different from the judgmental girls in my suite, then that's what I wanted to be!

My expectations of the institute, the leadership, and the friends I had hoped to make crumbled as the days went by. Even now I remember the pain of the disillusionment and disappointment in the lack of authentic Christian living and loving that I had observed. I wonder if Hagar had a similar jolting dose of reality.

Hagar had no way of knowing that she had entered into a wounded family. To have a wounded family, it stands to reason that there has to be someone who inflicts the pain. A "wounder." Abraham, the friend of God, the founding patriarch of the nation of Israel, the father of the faithful, was not only himself a wounder, but he was also married to one. Sarah was a woman in pain whose woundedness led her to wound others.

Abraham and Sarah truly loved each other but they had no children. For many years they carried the deep hurt that only childless couples really know. Abraham desperately wanted a son, someone to whom he could pass on all that he knew and owned. Sarah wanted a child just as desperately, not only for her own fulfillment, but to ease the shame that barrenness carried in her culture. In addition to her own reasons for wanting a child, she no doubt desired to give to her beloved husband the son he longed for. By the time Abraham and Sarah acquired Hagar, the pain of infertility had already laid the groundwork for a devastating cycle of wounds.

I wonder ... when did it first occur to Sarah that she had an ingenious solution to the pain in their lives? Perhaps the more she thought it through, the more logical it seemed. She knew God had promised Abraham a son, but God had not said the son would also be hers. Maybe, just maybe, God was waiting for her to do something. Surely, she thought, God helps those who help themselves anyway. And since she was past the age for childbearing — which in her mind meant the child God had promised Abraham could not possibly be her biological child — maybe there was another solution. A way out of their pain. A way to fulfill their lifelong dream and at the same time have what God promised — a child.

Sarah's solution? A surrogate mother! It must have seemed like a brilliant idea. Maybe she even wondered why she hadn't thought of it before. All of her neighbors followed the accepted custom of that day and used a servant to have the children they were unable to have, much like the way many couples use a surrogate mother to have children today. So Sarah's heart must have quickened a beat, and her eyes must have flashed with eager anticipation as she went to Abraham and shared her proposal: "The LORD has kept me from having children. Go, sleep with my maidservant; perhaps I can build a family through her."[1] And that's when the cycle of pain went into its next rotation because, "Abram agreed to what Sarai said.... He slept with Hagar, and she conceived."[2]

Neither Abraham or Sarah consulted God. Deep down, they must have known what He would say about this adulterous solution. While using a surrogate to have children may have been common practice among their peers, God's Word had clearly stated from the beginning that marriage was between one man and one woman.[3] While the Bible doesn't condemn Abraham and Sarah for what they did, it does let the story unfold, showing us that to go outside of God's principles is never a solution to a problem. It actually makes matters worse. In this case, while they may have gained some temporary relief from their pain, they made their lives much more complicated. Within a short period of time the home that had been filled with love and peace echoed with the sound of angry voices. Relationships were strained to the breaking point. More wounds were layered on top of their previous ones. And neither of them considered how this would possibly wound Hagar. How would she feel about being used as a surrogate to bear Abraham's child? So many wounds are inflicted almost without thinking, aren't they? We never sin unto ourselves. Sin invariably involves others, usually affecting those who are closest to us.

When Hagar became pregnant, perhaps her wounds weren't initially apparent. As the one who now carried Abraham's baby, her position in the household must have been greatly elevated. But then ...! Did she come to the startling conclusion that she, not Sarah, would be the one to give this great man what he had always dreamed of ... a son? The thought must have exploded in her mind ... *Oh, my goodness. I'm carrying The Child of promise!* Did it begin to occur to her that she now had exceptional value in the household? Value that she could barter for better treatment. A more exalted position. A more luxurious tent. Servants of her own. Did her Egyptian upbringing surface in her attitude as she became arrogant and self-centered? Did her tone of voice drip with condescension when she spoke to Sarah? Did she raise her eyebrows, look down her nose, toss her hair, and dismiss her mistress as an inferior nuisance? Was she no longer quick to serve, but slow and resentful at being asked to do anything? However Hagar expressed her superior attitude, we know that the happiness over her pregnancy was very short-lived because, "When she knew she was pregnant, she began to despise her mistress."[4] Hagar obviously was of the opinion that her ability to conceive made her somehow better than Sarah.

Hagar's arrogance and growing belly must have been like salt poured into the deep wounds of Sarah's raw and tender heart. The baby might legally belong to her since Hagar was her servant, but the child would never really be hers. Sarah was still barren and profoundly wounded. In her pain and with understandable outrage, she lashed out at Abraham, who wilted in the face of his wife's wrath. And then she lashed out at Hagar.[5]

Wounded people can very quickly become wounders, can't they? I learned this lesson in a dramatic way when I was a young girl. When my older sister left home to go to school, I inherited her toy silver poodle, Cedric, and we very quickly became inseparable. Cedric slept with me at night, stayed right beside me every waking minute, sat beside me at mealtimes, walked me to the front door in the morning when I went to school, and waited at the door to welcome me home when I returned in the afternoon. I loved that little dog!

One afternoon, my father's aide, Doug, came to take me to an appointment. I ran out the door and jumped into the car, forgetting to secure Cedric inside the house before I left. As we started down the steep, curving mountain driveway, I looked out the window and was horrified to see that Cedric was running to catch me! I urged Doug to stop the car so I could get Cedric, but instead, he thought he could just go faster and lose him. Within moments, I heard the dreaded bump-bump underneath the car and knew we had run over my little friend. Doug stopped the car and I jumped out. Sure enough, Cedric was lying crumpled in the driveway. I rushed to gather him in my arms, only to draw back in pain and confusion when he fiercely growled and sunk his teeth deep into my hand — to the bone. And he would not let go. I had to shake him off hard to free my hand. Now we were both hurt and bleeding. Cedric was whimpering and I was sobbing!

I wrapped his broken little body in my jacket, carefully staying clear of his teeth as we rushed him to the vet. Later, with my wound cleaned and bandaged, I asked my mother why Cedric had turned on me. "Anne," she replied, "Cedric was in pain. And when animals are in pain, you must be very careful about going near them because their pain can cause them blindly to lash out."

I have never forgotten the lesson. Wounded animals, whether four-legged or two-legged, can become wounders when hurt. Fortunately, like Cedric, we can also recover from our blinded-by-pain "biting." Though my little friend ultimately succumbed to complications from internal injuries a year after the accident, he remained steadfastly loyal and loving toward me to the day he died.

Perhaps the most extreme, literal example of the wounded becoming wounders is those who self-mutilate with a behavior known as cutting. People who suffer from this disorder regularly cut themselves in an attempt to release pent-up anger, fear, shame, guilt, and anxiety. They use physical pain to release emotional pain. Among the most prominent individuals who have struggled publicly with cutting is the late Princess Diana. In a BBC interview, she acknowledged cutting herself with a serrated lemon slicer, a pen knife, and razor blades. Explaining what drove her and others to harm themselves, she said, "You have so much pain inside yourself that you try and hurt yourself on the outside because you want help."

Hurting people hurt people. And often the one who seems to get "cut" the most is the person lashing out. They nurse their pain, anger, bitterness, frustration, unforgiveness, or resentment until those emotions become their master and they are enslaved to them. They are dominated by what Jesus described as "anger without a cause"[6] — anger that can erupt in a blind rage that has nothing at all to do with the person in the immediate vicinity, but is pent-up anger boiling over from within. While the eruption may bring temporary relief from the pain, the sad truth is that the "cutting" doesn't make them feel better for long. In fact, they can plunge into another type of "cutting" — self-flagellation for their uncontrollable behavior. Like picking at a scab on a physical wound, they relive again and again the situations that were so hurtful, holding imaginary conversations that never seem to end, living with the feeling of guilt that accompanies their wounding, desperately wishing they could have a do-over.

When we are wounded we need to be very careful about what happens next. Because in the aftermath we are vulnerable to the enemy of our souls who would seek to use us to wound others. Watch out!

There is no question that Sarah was hurting. And when she was wounded on top of her hurt, she very quickly responded by becoming a wounder.

Can you relate to Princess Diana or Sarah? Have you tried to release your pain through more pain? It doesn't work, does it? Wounding, at best, only temporarily releases pain. It may feel good for a few moments, hours, or days, but then it actually magnifies and perpetuates the pain. It keeps the cycle rotating in ever-widening circles that can impact generations yet to come. So what's the God-honoring alternative?

Many years after Abraham and Sarah and Hagar, the Bible tells us of another woman who carried the same deep hurt that Sarah had carried. Like Sarah, she was barren. And, also like Sarah, she was deeply and repeatedly wounded in that very same place of hurt. Her name was Hannah.

Hannah was Elkanah's second wife. Her Hagar, or antagonist, was Peninnah, her husband's first wife, who mercilessly ridiculed Hannah for her inability to conceive and bear a child. Peninnah "kept provoking her in order to irritate her — year after year — until she wept and would not eat." Depressed and almost non-functioning, Hannah described herself as a woman "who is deeply troubled."[7] Her pain was obvious, but how did she respond to Peninnah? Did she retaliate? Did she at least lash out verbally? Did she attack and blame Elkanah for allowing this to take place within his home?

No. None of the above. The way Hannah dealt with her pain stands in stark contrast to the way Sarah handled hers. Hannah's reaction gives us a beautiful and very moving picture of an alternative response to wounding that is available to all of God's children.

Hannah prayed. In her own words, she explained, "I was pouring out my soul to the LORD ... I have been praying here out of my great anguish and grief."[8] Hannah refused to become a wounder. The cycle of pain stopped when she chose to pray rather than retaliate. She prayed until she felt confirmed that God had heard her prayer. When she felt confirmed, immediately her depression lifted, and "she went her way and ate something, and her face was no longer downcast."[9]

Instead of experiencing another rotation in the cycle of pain, Hannah was blessed beyond measure! God miraculously answered her prayer and gave her not only a very special son, Samuel, but He opened her womb so that she actually had three more sons and two daughters.[10] Hannah's refusal to be a wounder resulted in joy and delight and, ultimately, honor for her — not only in the eyes of her husband, friends, and future generations, but also in the eyes of Peninnah, her rival and tormentor.[11]

When you are wounded, especially when the wound is inflicted on a place in your heart that is already very tender, what long-term difference might it make if you chose to respond as Hannah did? I do know that if Sarah had chosen to pray rather than retaliate, not only would she have prevented a cycle of pain in her own family, but she may have come into the ultimate blessing God had reserved for her much sooner than she did. As a result of taking matters into her own hands, she actually delayed for thirteen years God's supreme blessing of giving birth to her own son.

Sarah chose to respond to being wounded by becoming a wounder when Hagar's arrogance and impudence triggered an avalanche of rage that poured forth from her wounded heart. She buried Abraham in an emotional tsunami that caused him to throw up his hands and relinquish all responsibility: "Do with her whatever you think best."[12] Then he walked away.

What Sarah obviously thought best was to hurt Hagar as badly as Hagar had hurt her: "Then Sarai mistreated Hagar."[13] While the Bible doesn't tell us how Sarah mistreated Hagar, we can easily imagine. Did she verbally abuse her, belittling Hagar by saying she would never amount to anything? Did Sarah strike Hagar or confine her to the servants' quarters with only bread and water? Did she retaliate by forcing Hagar to muck out the camels' stalls in addition to her household chores? While we can only guess at what actually transpired between them, we do know that Sarah, praised in the New Testament as an exemplary woman of faith, wounded Hagar.

Before we raise our own eyebrows and pass judgment on Sarah, how many of us, dear reader, have wounded someone else? It's sad and shameful to admit, but even those we would consider exemplary men and women of faith wound others. I know.

Several years ago, a dearly beloved young friend gave her time and energy to hosting me for several strategic ministry events in her city. She did an outstanding job not only of organizing her community so that each event was filled to capacity with eager men and women, but also of emceeing the events themselves. She hosted the meetings with grace and poise as she clearly articulated that our aim was to revive the hearts of God's people. As she made the necessary public announcements, she also promoted my resources that were available at a table in the back of the room. I knew her reasoning was that each item that was offered was one that would help those who purchased it go deeper into God's Word. While I had no doubt that her motive was pure, I felt that she could have been misunderstood by some who might have been led to think we were using the meetings to make money off of my resources. So when I stepped into the pulpit, I intended to clarify what she said. But I handled it badly. In being sensitive to the audience, I was insensitive to my dear friend when I downplayed the resources, saying that they were not as important as getting into God's Word for yourself. However I worded it, it came across as a correction.

It wasn't until that evening when our ministry initiatives were completed that I became aware of how deeply hurt my friend was. By me. Early the next morning I called and asked if I could see her. She agreed. When I walked into her office, I saw the pain in her eyes and the downcast look on her face. I knew the only reason I could have hurt her to the extent that I had was that she loved and respected me. I took a deep breath, swallowed hard, and told her how sorry I was. To my dismay, she didn't accept my apology readily. Immediately, I learned a hard lesson. Wounded people may not get over their wounds easily or quickly. Wounds can be hard just to brush aside because the wounder says, "I'm sorry." But I persisted, desperate to recapture the warm relationship that had meant so much to me. So I talked through with her what I had said, and she explained how she had perceived it. I explained why I had said it and listened to her counter with why I shouldn't have said it. In the end, all I could do was say I was sorry. Which I was. All she could do was say she forgave me. Which she did. Then we moved on. We remain wonderful friends to this day.

I wonder what difference it would have made if Sarah had simply said she was sorry. Or if Hagar had said she was sorry. What difference would it have made if they had taken the time to talk things through and explain how each had hurt the other? But they didn't. Neither of them apologized. While it may have given Sarah temporary satisfaction and even pleasure to strike out at Hagar, the cycle of pain began to turn in her family and in Hagar's, and it is still turning today. The contemporary conflict between the Jewish state of Israel and her surrounding Arab neighbors, which has resulted in repeated physical, emotional, political, and psychological wounding, can be traced right back to this beginning of the cycle. That adds up to over four thousand years and untold billions of wounds!

Wounds can be contagious. One wound can divide and multiply as though it's a living cell, until entire families are taking sides, fighting, suing, not speaking to each other. Does that describe your family? Or your spouse's family? What misery we can inflict on each other. And families make up nations that actually take up arms and go to war over ... what? Wounds. And retaliatory wounding from past generations that have been passed down until regional conflicts seem to have no peaceful or diplomatic solution because the opposing sides just want to hurt each other.

The examples come so readily to mind, don't they? The conflict in the Balkans; the ongoing conflict in the Middle East; the generational animosity between Russia and her neighbors, between Iran and Iraq, between Japan and China, between the Hutus and Tutsis in Rwanda, between the Sunni and Shia Muslims, between African-Americans and Anglo-Americans, to name just a few — all can be traced back to wounds and wounding and entire generations that have taken up the war cry. It would be safe to assume that some of those fighting today don't even know why they are fighting or how or when the conflict started. They are just steeped in hatred that was birthed in pain long before they entered the world. Then they are taught by parents, grandparents, siblings, political leaders, and religious institutions to hate ... just because.

Would the contagious cycle of pain in your life, or that of your family or church, be stopped if you would be the first to reach out, to give in, to say you are sorry, or at the very least open up a conversation on the source of the wounds? You may never know the difference it would make until you do.

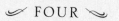

FOUR

The Believer in Exile

*Running from
the Wounders*

Sarai mistreated Hagar; so she fled from her.

Genesis 16:6

One of the more difficult experiences my husband, Danny, and I have had took place in a church that he helped plant. After four years of meeting with a group of men to pray regularly for God's leadership and blessing, he joined them as they incorporated into a church body. He served the church as both an adult Sunday school teacher and an elder. Once the church was established, the elders interviewed and then called a young seminary professor named Steve to serve as senior pastor. He accepted the call, and everyone was thrilled. He was passionate about the Word and had a heart to bring people to salvation through the Gospel. His preaching was solid, his demeanor was confident, and the church began to grow. For about three months.

Then Steve had a terrible motorcycle accident that landed him in the hospital for weeks. That's when the whispering campaign began, instigated by those who had decided Steve was not the pastor they had envisioned for the church. They used his absence to foster dissatisfaction: *Do you like Steve's preaching? Don't you think his messages have been a little hard to understand? Don't you think he missed the main point of chapter such and such?*

As I listened to what members were saying and what my husband related concerning the discussion behind the closed doors of the elder meetings, I knew momentum was building to remove this young pastor from his position. The astounding reason the whispers were so effective was that the primary instigators of the gossip were two prominent Bible teachers in the church. They succeeded in sowing doubt and dissatisfaction about Steve in the hearts and minds of many of the people because the people trusted and loved them.

What followed was months of almost nightly elder meetings that functioned more like a kangaroo court than a group of faithful men seeking God's will. When my husband resisted the efforts to remove Steve from leadership, the wife of a prominent elder was assigned to pay us a house call. She wept as she tried to convince us that Steve was not the right person for the job and therefore needed to be removed. Our response was that the church had called Steve and, unless there was a moral, ethical, or theological reason for his removal, we would stand by him. She disagreed, and we had to ask her to leave our home.

In the end, with my husband as the only elder who stood his ground firmly beside the wounded young pastor, Steve was forced to resign.

While the people who attended the church were good people, they did not know what had taken place behind closed doors. Steve's departure was publicly spun as a desire on his part to return to full-time seminary teaching. His farewell dinner was accompanied by praise and prayers and a generous severance package. The cover-up worked for the congregation, who had no reason to believe otherwise. They simply seemed grateful that the pastor they had been led to believe was not God's choice for their church was leaving of his own volition.

When Steve left, so did Danny and I. For one year, we did not attend any church. Once again, we found ourselves on the outside. The first time was years before when Danny's leadership had been rejected by the applauding congregation. This time it was when we felt we needed to support Steve and take a stand for what we felt was fair, ethical, biblical, and Christlike. I was not bitter, angry, or vengeful. Just heartbroken. I wrote a letter to each of the seven elders at the church explaining our position and asking for reconciliation. I never received even one response. And so we simply chose to separate ourselves. We became believers in exile.

Are you in exile also? Have you been rejected or refused? Slighted or slandered? Betrayed or backstabbed? Demonized or divorced? Abandoned or accused? Passed-over or pushed-out? Wounded! *By God's people!*

As a result have you just walked out? Out of church, out of any religious organization or denomination, out of that relationship, out of that family, out of that ministry, out of that job? Are you running from the wounders right into exile? If so, I understand.

As a result of our own experience of being believers in exile, I have been alert to others who find themselves in a similar situation. One such person who came to my attention is a gifted Bible teacher, raised in the church because her father was the pastor, yet who now does not belong to any church. For church, she has substituted a small group that meets in various homes. Another believer in exile is a well-known Christian author who does not attend church regularly but floats from one circle of Christian friends to another. When I shared with him the subject of this book, he confirmed the need for me to write it. He shared that many of his friends are in the same situation he is. They are committed Christians, but have been so burned by the organized church that they no longer feel they can be comfortable in it. They are in exile.

While working on this book, I went to visit my father. I had fixed dinner for him, and as he so often does following the meal, he invited me to share a devotional thought with him and others who were in the house. I read from the Bible and then opened up the time for discussion.

One lovely young woman made a few comments that provoked my query, "Where do you go to church?" Her eyes flickered, and I knew I was looking at someone who had been wounded. She shared that she and her husband had been actively involved in their church. They had taught the young people, led the youth retreats, become best friends of the pastor and his wife, and were included in the church staff functions. Then her husband suddenly left her. Just walked out. As she shared her story, it wasn't the memory of being abandoned that caused her tears to flow; it was the fact that not one person on the church staff or in the church at large had reached out to her. No one had called, come by, dropped her a note, or just asked her how she was doing. Not one.

"So, I don't go to church anymore," she whispered.

She has become a believer in exile.

What propelled you into exile? Who wounded you? Was it a co-worker who berated you? An in-law who ridiculed you? A spouse who abused you? A boss who humiliated you? A child who defied you? Or _____? You fill in the blank.

And were the only ones who could have come to your aid so intimidated or indifferent that they just threw up their hands and walked away, leaving you defenseless — just as Hagar was left defenseless by Abraham? How did it make you feel?

Not long ago, a beautiful older woman described to me her experience of being left defenseless. Doctors who misdiagnosed her illness as drug addiction had locked her in a psychiatric ward to force her off her medications — and they did so with her husband's consent.

Two days later, the same doctors released her when the actual cause of her illness was identified. It was not drug addiction. As she shared the traumatic experience of being misdiagnosed and committed against her will, her voice was hoarse with emotion as she said, "And my husband stood by and allowed it."

Have you been wounded while someone who could have intervened and prevented it didn't? Did your sibling steal your inheritance from one parent while your other parent allowed it in order to avoid confrontation? Did a church staff member remove you from your volunteer ministry responsibilities while your senior pastor said he or she couldn't override the chain of authority in the church? Did a co-worker steal credit for your project while your manager remained silent to avoid rocking the boat? Did your former spouse verbally berate you while your present spouse said it wasn't his or her place to interfere? It hurts, doesn't it?

When our beloved only son was going through the trauma and pain of a divorce, on several occasions his emotions became so raw they were volatile. He had been deeply wounded, and in his pain he lashed out. On one particular occasion, the house reverberated with the sound of his angry words that had been directed primarily at me. My husband, his father, witnessed the explosion, but sat silently throughout it. He then got up and walked out of the room. At that moment, I had no support, no defender, no protector. And it hurt.

While every parent experiences those moments when the other parent does not step up so that one is left to deal alone with whatever the situation is, it still hurts, doesn't it? All I knew to do was to cry out to God.

In reflecting on other hurtful times when I have been mistreated and left defenseless, I will admit that I haven't always prayed first.

My responses have covered almost the entire spectrum. While I have prayed, I have also wept. I have tried to hit back. I have sharpened the sword of my tongue and given it back as fiercely as it was given to me. I have been speechless. I have spoken softly. I have spoken forcefully in self-defense. I have immediately apologized. And there have been times when I've tried my best to extricate myself from the situation and do everything possible to avoid that person in the future, which is a form of running away. How have you responded to your hurt? At times, running away seems like our only recourse for self-protection.

Hagar responded to her hurt by running away. When Abraham gave Sarah permission to do what she wanted with her servant and then walked away in apparent indifference, Hagar must have felt like she'd taken a knife wound to the heart. And so it's not surprising that she responded by running.

Hagar also responded with what I'm sure she considered self-defense — a large dose of self-pity as she ran. She must have seen herself as a victim, a servant forced to do what Abraham and Sarah told her to do. When Abraham left her at Sarah's mercy, Hagar must have thought, *I'm not going to stay around and take this. The pagans back in Egypt treated me better than these so-called "godly" people. I'll just go back to Egypt.* So Hagar, carrying Abraham's unborn child, ran away. But when she ran away from hurt and humiliation, she also ran away from God's people, God's presence, and God's promises. And I wonder … was she also running away from God? Because if Sarah was any reflection of what He was like, it would have been understandable if Hagar had decided she never wanted to know Him.

Whatever the circumstances of your wounding may be, don't make Hagar's mistake. Don't blame God for the behavior of the people who have wounded you. I understand the desperate desire to run from *them*, but not from *Him*. Besides, running away never really solves anything, does it? It just delays dealing with whatever or whomever it is you are running from.

As tragically self-defeating as it is, many other wounded people seem to follow Hagar in her decision to flee into exile. Recently, I read an article about bestselling novelist, Anne Rice.[1] Ms. Rice had come to faith in a much talked-about conversion that she described in her book *Called Out of Darkness: A Spiritual Confession*. The article included this quote from the author's Facebook page:

> For those who care, and I understand if you don't: Today I quit being a Christian. I'm out. I remain committed to Christ as always but not to being a "Christian" or to being part of Christianity … It's simply impossible for me to "belong" to this quarrelsome, hostile, disputatious, and deservedly infamous group. For ten years, I've tried. I've failed. I'm an outsider. My conscience will allow nothing else.

If the words of Anne Rice are heart-wrenching to me, and they are, I can only imagine how her words and her decision must grieve the God of Hagar. I sincerely pray that God will find Ms. Rice in exile. That's where He found Hagar. God cared about Hagar, and He cares about Anne Rice. God cares about those who are running from the pain. Running from the problem. Running from God's people. Running from the wounders. And yes, God cares about you. Even if you are running from Him.

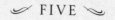

FIVE

God Cares

You Can't Outrun God

The angel of the LORD *found Hagar near a spring in the desert; it was the spring that is beside the road to Shur. And he said, "Hagar ..."*

Genesis 16:7 – 8

In the previous chapter I described the church situation that sent my husband and me into exile. But let me continue the story, because although we "ran" from the church, we couldn't outrun God.

The same day my husband and I left the church, the telephone rang. A young pastor named Marc was calling from a distant state. He had been a friend to our children when they were all in college together, had been in our home, and had become our friend as well. We hadn't heard from him in years, so his phone call was a delightful surprise. After catching up with personal news, Marc told Danny the purpose for his call. He wanted to tell us about a good friend of his named Scott who had served as an intern at the same large church where Marc was a pastor. He described Scott as a gifted preacher who had a heart for evangelism and wanted to plant a church in our area. Marc, who knew nothing of our church situation, then asked Danny if he would be willing to show Scott around our community. Much to my dismay, Danny agreed.

After forty years of practicing dentistry in our city and forty-five years of being involved in several large parachurch organizations, my husband knew just about every Christian of influence in our area. So while I was glad for him to open doors for the young pastor and introduce him to some key people, I wanted no part of it. The last thing I wanted to do was to get involved in another church plant, so I stayed clear of Scott.

But the more time Danny spent with Scott, and the more he

listened to Scott's heart and vision, the more excited he became about helping him start a church — and the more skeptical I became. Finally, I felt I had no choice. I agreed to meet Scott, his wife, and their newborn daughter, but I had every intention of squelching my husband's enthusiasm. Over lunch, I asked Scott some fairly pointed questions: What was his conversion experience? When was the last time he personally led someone to faith in Jesus Christ? Why did he want to plant a church in our area? What did he hope to accomplish in a region where there is a church on every street corner? What would be unique about the church he wanted to start?

Scott answered with humility, boldness, confidence, clarity of vision, and purpose — and the more he talked, the more I sensed God's hand was on his life. At the end of that first conversation, my eyes were opened to something I believed God was doing, and my resistance melted. I agreed with Danny to do whatever we could to help Scott. One year to the day after going into exile, Danny and I returned. We came back into church fellowship with those who are not perfect but are committed to connecting people to Jesus for life change. Because God cares, He brought us out of exile.

Although Hagar was not aware of it, God cared about her also as she ran from her wounders. As her sandaled feet moved swiftly over the rough, rocky terrain that emptied into an endless desert, I imagine she must have felt lonely, confused, terrified, and angry. I expect she mentally replayed the scene with Sarah over and over again. Maybe she even had an imaginary confrontation: *Just who do you think you are? Your name might mean "princess," but you're nothing but a bitter, barren old woman. As for sleeping with your husband, do you think I enjoyed that for even one moment? I was just doing my duty. Now I'm carrying his child, which is more than you could ever say. And you'd better not follow me or I'll run and run and keep on running until I'm so far away you will never find me. And the old man will never have his baby.*

One reason I think Hagar may have had an imaginary confrontation with Sarah is that I often rehearse imaginary conversations with my wounders, honing my words like knives on flint until they are not only sharp, but seem brilliant to me. Of course, as my words get sharper and sharper, I find myself feeling angrier and more justified in self-pity or in plotting revenge. Although I would never speak the words out loud, they shred my inner peace because they keep my focus on "them," and what they did to me.

Instead of having an imaginary conversation with myself, I would be better served by pouring out my heart to God in prayer. Yet I have discovered that while I may have an endless supply of angry words for a one-sided conversation in my mind, I find myself at a deplorable loss for words in prayer. When that happens and I struggle for words, I often turn to David's prayers in the Psalms and use them as my own. For example,

> Give ear to my words, O LORD,
>   consider my sighing.
> Listen to my cry for help,
>   my King and my God,
>   for to you I pray.
> In the morning, O LORD, you hear my voice;
>   in the morning I lay my requests before you
>   and wait in expectation....
> The arrogant cannot stand in your presence;
>   you hate all who do wrong.

You destroy those who tell lies....
Lead me, O LORD, in your righteousness
   because of my enemies —
   make straight your way before me.
Not a word from their mouth can be trusted....
   Let their intrigues be their downfall....
But let all who take refuge in you be glad;
   let them ever sing for joy.
Spread your protection over them,
   that those who love your name may rejoice in you.
For surely, O LORD, you bless the righteous;
   you surround them with your favor as with a shield.[1]

David's honesty in his prayers resonates with my heart. Often he begins his prayer complaining, crying out, expressing anger toward his enemies, but invariably he ends his prayer with praise of God. You can almost pinpoint the place where his focus changes from "them" to "Him."

I know by experience what David knew. Prayer can help heal your hurt. It can take the sting away. One reason is that it can help put your wounding in perspective. When I focus on God and who He is, my wounders don't seem so intimidating and my hurt somehow becomes smaller. So may I encourage you? Put the brakes on any runaway mental conversations you may be having with those who have wounded you. If you don't, and those sharp words career recklessly across the highway of your healing journey, your wounded heart and life are going to end up as something like splattered roadkill. At the very least, you will delay, and perhaps even deny, the healing God wants to give you. And while the damage may not be readily apparent to anyone else, you will miss out on the blessing and purpose God has for you.

Maybe you are not having any imaginary conversations — no one-sided, mental confrontations with your wounders. Instead, maybe you are having *actual* conversations ... but with others, not with the ones who hurt you. Perhaps you have gravitated to people who have also been wounded. As you repeatedly open your wounds to sympathetic ears, you begin to feel not only supported and encouraged, but also justified in your hardness of heart. It's as though your deterioration into a bitter, angry person is not only something you can blame on the wounder, but also a means of revenge. You want others to know how bad that person has been by showing them how miserable you are. It reminds me of an old saying: "Bitterness is like drinking poison hoping the other person gets sick."

Who have you invited to "drink the poison" with you? How long is the guest list for your pity party? Are you gathering an audience to listen to your angry complaints, witness your heated tears, and stir up the same outrage you feel for the offender? Unfortunately, pity parties never result in authentic benefit or blessing; they just enlarge, deepen, and intensify the wound by repeatedly exposing it. At the very least, these kinds of discussions with others will keep you focused on your hurts instead of focused on your Healer.

Hagar's focus was definitely not on her Healer. She was running. And she was running on "the road to Shur."[2] That was the road to Egypt. Hagar was going back. Back home to her mother. Back home to the familiar pagans of Egypt. Back home to where she used to belong. She reminds me of the apostle Peter, who went back to his prior life of fishing after his dismal failure as a disciple when he denied his Lord.[3]

When we fail at trying to do the right thing, or live the right way, or say the right words, or be the right person, or fit into the right fellowship, we often just want to give up and say, "I can't do this. I'm going back to the life I used to know." The familiarity of a former way of life, or old friends, or previous habits can seem to be comfortable at a time when we're rejected or wounded by God's people. The "world" of Egypt seems safer than the "church" of Abraham's tent. But going back only increases our misery, doesn't it? We can't go back. Not really. Because we can remember what it was like to be in God's presence and to be part of His family with a greater purpose to life than just living for ourselves. Yet we find ourselves in a Catch-22. We don't really want to go back to our former way of life, but we don't feel we fit in with God's people either. Which is why God Himself needs to show up.

It was at this miserable moment on the road to Shur as Hagar was not only running away, but running back, that God showed up and taught her a profound life lesson: *Even if you run from the wounders, you can't outrun God.*

As she ran, her heart must have been beating out of her chest. Her breath must have come in shallow gasps, either from the physical exertion or the panic she surely experienced when "the angel of the LORD found Hagar near a spring in the desert."[4]

God did show up! Hagar wasn't alone after all. He was there. Right there. Because God cares. He came to her as "the angel of the LORD," a mysterious description of Him as He appears suddenly, unexpectedly, and seemingly out of nowhere from time to time in the Old Testament. God is described as the Angel of the Lord when He wrestled with Jacob by the Jabbok River, leaving him both blessed and limping.[5] He was described in a similar fashion when He confronted

Joshua outside of Jericho, told him to take off his shoes because he was on holy ground, and then told him how to overcome the enemy fortress.[6] He appeared to Gideon in this way, appointing him as the deliverer of His people when he was hiding from the Midianites in the winepress.[7] Again and again this intriguing figure appears throughout the history of Israel. Scholars agree that the Angel of the Lord is a "theophany," or an appearance of the pre-incarnate Son of God. Astoundingly, He is Jesus before Bethlehem! Who can fathom the magnificent grace of God in that the very first time we encounter the visible Son of God is right here, at the spring beside the road to Shur, revealing Himself . . .

> to a woman not a man;
>
> to a servant, not a warrior;
>
> to an Egyptian, not a descendant of Abraham;
>
> to a sinner, not a saint;
>
> to a slave, not a king;
>
> to an outsider, not an insider.

What an undeserved, compassionate intervention of the Creator in the life of one wounded woman. He intentionally sought and found her — while she was running!

Why? Why did God go after Hagar? Why didn't He just let her run away, die in the desert, have a timely miscarriage, or return to Egypt where she would never have been heard from again? Having Hagar out of the picture would have solved a lot of problems in Abraham's household. So why didn't God simply dismiss her as Abraham had done?

The incredibly wonderful, amazing answer is because God loved Hagar! God felt her pain even though it was provoked by her own arrogance. He cared so much about the wounds inflicted on a pregnant Egyptian servant that He left His throne in heaven and ran after her, pursuing her right into the desert. While God chose Abraham as the one through whom He would uniquely bless the world, Hagar represented the world that He wanted to bless.

God loved Hagar as much as He loved Abraham!

This is a truth to wrap your heart and mind around, especially in a world that sometimes thinks God cares more about ...

Jews than Muslims,

whites than blacks,

the churched than the unchurched,

insiders than outsiders,

men than women,

rich people than poor people,

adults than children,

religious people than atheists;

that He cares more about *us* than *them*.

God cares about each of us and all of us — period! And because He really does love you — He really does care about you — you and I can run, but we can't *outrun* Him.

When Hagar knelt to get a refreshing drink from the spring, she heard a sound. It may have taken a few moments to quiet her racing heart and collect her scattered thoughts so she could really listen. It must have been a sound more beautiful than gurgling water, clearer than a singing bird, softer than the desert wind, more tender than her mother's voice.

Glancing in the direction of the sound, her eyes must have squinted against the harsh, glaring light of the sun, trying to focus through her tears on who was speaking to her. Then she saw Him. A mysterious figure gazing at her with a compassion that reached back before the foundations of the world, reached ahead all the way to the cross, reached up all the way to heaven, and reached down to her — right there — on the desert road that led to Egypt.

He was speaking to her, calling her by name. *Hagar . . .*

And the little wounded runaway servant girl, with tears streaming down her grimy face, her heart still pumping furiously, her breath coming in ragged gasps, encountered the One Who Sees and pursues those who are running. She met the amazing God David worshiped and to whom David prayed:

> Where can I go from your Spirit?
>> Where can I flee from your presence?
> If I go up to the heavens, you are there;
>> if I make my bed in the depths, you are there.
> If I rise on the wings of the dawn,
>> if I settle on the far side of the sea,
> even there your hand will guide me,
>> your right hand will hold me fast.[8]

Wherever you are, whoever you are, David's God — the God of Hagar — is right there. If you can still the racing beat of your heart, quiet your frantic thoughts, silence those imaginary conversations, listen carefully with the ears of your spirit, then you will begin to hear His voice. I think I can hear Him now, calling you by name . . .

SIX

Spiritual Blind Spots

*You Are Missing
the Obvious*

And he said, "Hagar, servant of Sarai, where have you come from, and where are you going?"

"I'm running away from my mistress Sarai," she answered.

Then the angel of the LORD told her, "Go back to your mistress and submit to her." The angel added, "I will so increase your descendants that they will be too numerous to count ..."

She gave this name to the LORD who spoke to her: "You are the God who sees me," for she said, "I have now seen the One who sees me." That is why the well was called Beer Lahai Roi; it is still there, between Kadesh and Bered.

So Hagar bore Abram a son, and Abram gave the name Ishmael to the son she had borne. Abram was eighty-six years old when Hagar bore him Ishmael.

Genesis 16:8 – 10, 13 – 16

Both of my parents have suffered from macular degeneration, a disease that blurs vision by causing a blind spot. My mother used to look at me with her characteristic twinkle and exclaim, "Anne, I can't see your face. All I can see is a blank spot framed with hair." In the end, she couldn't even see my hair! And in spite of the latest medical treatments, including frequent injections directly into his eye, my father has lost the ability to focus. He can no longer read his Bible or the daily newspapers that still come to the house. His wonderful staff has improvised so that they pull up a large flat-screen television within three feet of where he is sitting, but he still has difficulty seeing the picture. One of my joys when I visit is to watch TV with him, explaining what I see. Or to read the newspaper headlines to him, commenting on what I read and asking him what he thinks. I can't imagine how hard it is for my father, whose mind is still alert and active, to have blind spots that hinder him from seeing clearly.

Having witnessed the effects of this disease up close, I see it as the perfect metaphor for Hagar's spiritual condition when she fled from Abraham and Sarah. She suffered from a significant blind spot of her own, a kind of spiritual macular degeneration. There were some things she just could not see clearly. So the Angel of the Lord gently questioned her. Not for information, since He already knew what had happened. He questioned Hagar for her own benefit, to help her focus. He wanted Hagar to talk things through with Him because she may have thought that she was just a victim, not responsible for what had happened. That the mess she was in was someone else's fault. She may have been bitterly focused on *them* — God's people who had wronged her — while remaining blind to her own failures.

The Angel of the Lord gently probed her blindness: "Hagar, servant of Sarai, where have you come from, and where are you going?"[1] Reading between the lines, I can imagine a whole host of additional questions: *Hagar, will you talk with Me for a moment about what you're doing and where you belong? You are Sarah's servant; don't you think you belong with her? Are you sure this is what you want to do with your life and where you want to go? Is this really wise? Will this course of action make you happy? Hagar, I know you've been deeply hurt by people who call themselves by My name. You're rejecting them. Are you also rejecting Me? Let's think this through carefully. Together.*

When wounded, you and I also need to think things through very carefully. Could the wounding we've received be in response to wounds we've inflicted? It would be beneficial to talk things over with God because, if you're like me, it's easy to develop spiritual macular degeneration. When I'm hurt, it's so much easier to focus on the faults of others. It seems to be almost an instinctive reaction to wounding and a convenient defense mechanism: *It's not me. It's them! And even if it were me, what I did to them wasn't as hurtful as what they did to me. So it's still them!*

Like Hagar, we need help in focusing on ourselves. So I've paraphrased the questions that the Angel of the Lord used to probe her heart to make them more relevant and personal for us. Prayerfully consider answering them one by one ...

- Where are you in your healing journey?
- Do you remember what your life was like before you were wounded?

- How did you get to this place?
- How is the way you are reacting today going to help you tomorrow?
- Do you want your life characterized by the result of remaining focused on "them" while being blind to your own pride, arrogance, anger, resentment, name-calling, vengeful digs, schemes for revenge, or vicious gossip disguised as prayer requests?
- Are these attitudes working for you and making you happy?
- Do they give you a temporary sense of satisfaction but then disintegrate into a desire for even more revenge? And more misery?
- What are you living for? Instead of living your life to the glory of God, are you driven by a desire to get even, vindicate your actions, prove someone else wrong, justify your opinion, expose the other person, get your own way?
- Consider carefully … do any of these desires truly honor God?
- When was the last time you put your head on the pillow conscious of God's sweet peace and joy flooding your heart? If you can't remember, could it be time for you to give your attention to considering your own part in the wounding?

Some of those questions hurt. I know because I have asked them of myself before sharing them with you. It can seem less uncomfortable to keep our eyes shut when the light of truth reveals our blind spot than to open our eyes and allow the light to penetrate into the deep recesses of our hearts where we rarely go. It takes courage to endure that kind of pain and just open our eyes.

Hagar didn't open her eyes. Her response to the Lord's questions, while being honest, reveals that she was still out of focus. Her attention seemed to be more on Sarah than herself: "I'm running away from my mistress Sarai."[2] I can almost hear the unspoken subtext behind her words: *It's not my fault. Sarah is the cause of this. She's mean.*

While ignoring her own sin of arrogance, I wonder if Hagar's life then flashed before her mind's eye as she indulged in a full-scale pity party. Did all the old wounds pop up like boils on her heart? How Pharaoh had given her as chattel to Abraham and Sarah; how frightened and alone she had felt in the Canaanite wilderness; how she had tried but seemingly failed to please Sarah or fit into her new life; how unfair it was that she would never have her own husband and children; how she had been robbed of her innocence when Sarah commanded her to sleep with Abraham; how surreal it had been to discover she was carrying his baby; how she had taken advantage of the situation, knowing she was carrying Abraham's treasured heir; how she had despised and rebelled against Sarah for forcing her into motherhood before she was a wife; how Abraham, after impregnating her, had shown her such indifference and looked the other way when Sarah abused her; how Sarah had stripped her of her privileges, slapped her, and sent her back to the servants' quarters.

I'm sure that the more she thought about it, the more blurred her vision became. Reliving what Sarah had done to her kept Hagar blinded to what she had done to Sarah.

Are your spiritual eyes also squeezed tightly shut as you relive over and over again the hurtful actions or words that have wounded you? The memory of one impossible expectation or one infuriating expression, one unfair decision or one unreasonable demand, one injustice or one insult, one wound or one wrong, can bring back to our minds another one and another one until we are smothered in a nasty heap of ugliness that hardens our hearts and embitters our spirit and blinds us to the obvious — our own faults and sin.

It's both interesting and sad to think how easily you and I can see the faults in others while absolving ourselves of responsibility for what our actions or words may have provoked. Although Sarah's behavior could indeed have been characterized as mean, Hagar failed to acknowledge how her contempt and scorn had provoked Sarah.[3] When we are wounded, hurt feelings and injured pride can distort our perspective and our focus. In self-defense, we want to explain and excuse and blame the ones who wounded us. We want to prove our point — *I was right; they were wrong. How dare they treat me this way!* We tend to rationalize our own behavior while holding others to a standard we don't apply to ourselves. It's revealing to note that when we point a finger at someone else, we literally have three fingers pointing back at ourselves!

Jesus addressed this spiritual blindness in the Sermon on the Mount when He admonished the crowd: "Why do you look at the speck of sawdust in your brother's eye and pay no attention to the plank in your own eye? How can you say to your brother, 'Let me take the speck out of your eye,' when all the time there is a plank in your own eye? You hypocrite, first take the plank out of your own eye, and then you will see clearly to remove the speck from your brother's eye."[4]

When you and I focus on the speck of sin in the other person's life while paying no attention to the plank in our own, God will begin to get our attention. He may use a lack of peace, an absence of joy, an agitation of spirit, a knot in the pit of our stomachs, a dullness or depression in our emotions, or something else to alert us that we are not all right. Because God truly loves you and me, He won't let us get by with excuses, rationalizations, and self-defense. A spiritual blind spot is something He will seek to correct.

The correction can be hard to take when it comes through someone else. For myself, I want to give the Angel of the Lord my full attention in order for the correction to come from Him, not another person. In my experience, when it does come from Him, although it is specifically pinpointed, He opens my eyes of self-awareness quite gently and lovingly, yet firmly. There is no blame or condemnation. Just truth and light and assurance that as I confess and submit to His correction I am right with Him, and I have the hope that one day I will be right with others. He taught me this in a fresh way not too long ago ...

A lovely and longtime friend emailed me one day to set up a time when she could talk with me about something on her mind. She didn't tell me what it was, just that she needed some time to talk. I knew she was aware that I was going through a difficult time, both personally and in ministry. She had helped me with some ministry initiatives in the past, and the thought crossed my mind that perhaps she wanted to offer her assistance once again.

When we met, I embraced her warmly, and we spent twenty minutes or so just catching up as friends. She described a broken relationship between her siblings and how grieved she was at their unwillingness to forgive one another. I assured her I would pray for healing in her family relationships. Then I asked why she had wanted to meet with me. In tears, she explained that because I had hurt her in the past, she had made the decision not to help me with the ministry challenges I was currently facing. In fact, she said she could no longer help me in any way again. I was so caught off guard that I was stunned. She was effectively severing our relationship. At the moment I was incapable of doing anything except just sitting and staring at her, utterly speechless. While I had no words to respond, I was truly amazed by the irony. Because my friend could clearly see the sin of unforgiveness at work in the lives of her siblings, yet she seemed totally blind to her own unwillingness to forgive me for what she felt were past hurts. My mind reeled in confusion and consternation as I wondered what sin in my life I was blind to that had hurt her to such an extreme that she would take this action.

If my friend's purpose in meeting with me was to wound me as she felt I had wounded her, she succeeded. But what was really accomplished? Instead of continuing our conversation and seeking reconciliation, she broke our relationship, an action that I believe grieved the heart of God. And it was carried out within moments of requesting prayer for reconciliation in her own family. That's blindness. Spiritual macular degeneration.

I came away from that meeting more determined than ever to have my own eyes opened to the plank that must have been there. I couldn't help but wonder what I had done to wound her, and if I had wounded her so deeply, could it be I was also wounding others without knowing it? I did not, and do not, want to suffer from spiritual macular degeneration. Especially when it results in hurting someone else.

In spite of the fact that I want to "see," I've found it difficult, if not impossible, to open my own eyes. I know I have blind spots, but I just can't see them. Actually, that's why they are called blind spots. So this past year, following the meeting with my friend and in preparation for leading a revival, I decided to ask God to do for me what the Angel of the Lord did for Hagar. I asked Him to show me my blind spots. And He did. At least He showed me some of them. I am quite sure there are more.

When I asked God to shine the light of His truth deep into my heart, I had to make the time for Him to do so. Practically, this meant that I spent a significant portion of each and every day for about two months searching for anything that was not pleasing to Him. To help me focus, I used a spiral-bound book that had been given to me by a friend and was developed to deepen and enrich a believer's prayer life.[5] In the book were several lists: Names of sins. Categories of sins. Definitions of sins. Antidotes to sins. Confessions of sins. Forgiveness for sins with hundreds of Scripture references. It was exactly what I needed to help me see.

Because God is faithful and able to open the eyes of the blind, He answered my prayer. He opened my eyes as I read through the lists of sins ... meditating on just a few every day. When I worked my way through all of the lists, I went back and worked my way through them again. Then I did it for a third time. I can tell you it was not pleasant. It was not comfortable. In fact, it was painful and required courage even to look at myself the way God was revealing me to be in His eyes. But it was also deeply cleansing. And corrective. And very freeing.

While I won't share with you the various sins that God pinpointed in my life, I will share one, because I had been so totally blind to it. It was listed in the category of "control," which is sin that dishonors God's sovereignty. And there is was: *perfectionism*. It stopped me cold. I froze when my eyes came to it in my first reading of the list. I didn't need to read the list three times to know that was me. I'm a perfectionist. But I had never considered that to be a sin. In fact, I had thought it was a strength as it challenges me to strive for excellence, and in turn, I have challenged my family and those I work with to strive for excellence also. But what I had never seen is that my perfectionism, taken to the extreme, had been used to control others. While focused on the speck in the eyes of others, I had ignored the plank in my own. As my sin came clearly into focus, I immediately, earnestly confessed it and told the Lord how very sorry I was for having dishonored His sovereignty in such a manner. Then I humbly asked Him to heal those I had unconsciously wounded as a result.

Like me, and perhaps like you, Hagar had been focused on the speck of sawdust — Sarah's wrongdoing — while ignoring the plank of arrogance in her own life. So God's instructions to Hagar were clear, comforting, but corrective and firm: "Go back to your mistress and submit to her.... I will so increase your descendants that they will be too numerous to count."[6] In other words, *Hagar, the only way to resolve this entire mess is to refocus. You're missing the obvious. You're not responsible for "fixing" Sarah. She may never acknowledge that what she did to you was wrong. But you are responsible for your own words and behavior. You must turn around. Go back. Humble yourself. Face the consequences. If you do, Hagar, I will bless you, your son, your grandchildren, and your future generations immeasurably. I will give you an honored place in history. Because I not only care about your wound, Hagar, I care about you.*

Amazingly, Hagar did turn around. Not petulantly, reluctantly, or with hesitation, but with the joy of knowing that not just Abraham, but now *she herself* — an Egyptian slave — had a personal relationship with the living God, the Creator of the Universe! Her wounded heart was filled with the wonder of His grace and love and personal attention as she exclaimed, "You are the God who sees me

... I have now seen the One who sees me."[7] The blind spot was gone, and her vision was 20/20!

The Bible describes the turnaround as repentance. For me, like Hagar, it wasn't enough just to have a name for my blind spot. It wasn't enough to have had a fresh encounter with the One who sees me, inside and out. I had to turn around. While I did choose to repent, carrying through on that decision has been an ongoing effort as I work out the practical application. Because I'm still a perfectionist. But I have had to train myself to see the difference between excellence and control, giving those around me, including myself, the freedom to fail and fall short of my standards. I find myself continually tested on my willingness to let go of control while still lifting up the standard of excellence. They are tests that, by God's grace and power, I want to pass. One by one. Day by day. Until I overcome the sin that has been so blinding. But to pass those tests, I must be willing to turn around. To repent of my sin. To stop it.

What about you? Have you acknowledged your sin that you now see, but you have yet to turn around? Until you are willing to repent of your sin, you will never overcome it. And you will miss the blessing that God has for you. Repentance is vital if you and I are to successfully continue on our journey to healing.

Wounded people need to repent of their sin. And the wounders need to repent also. Sarah herself had suffered from a severe case of spiritual macular degeneration. One can only imagine the look on her face when Hagar returned. Consternation. Anger. Guilt. Misery. I wonder if the shock of seeing Hagar jolted Sarah's vision so that she also began to see more clearly. She had been the one who suggested to Abraham that he have a child by Hagar. Yet when Hagar became pregnant and arrogantly despised her barren mistress, Sarah illogically, unreasonably, and blindly pointed an accusing finger at Abraham: "You are responsible for the wrong I am suffering."[8] Sarah blamed her husband for a situation she herself had arranged! It might seem ludicrous if it wasn't so much like what all of us do when we allow our wounds to blind us. That's the most striking characteristic of a blind spot — it can be easily seen by everyone ... except ourselves.

Sarah must have thought she could easily get rid of her problem with just a sharp word and the slap of her hand. But when Hagar returned, Sarah no doubt had to do some serious soul-searching and heart-cleansing and sin-repenting of her own. For the next fifteen years or so, we don't hear anything about her or from her. She slips into the background of Abraham's life and appears to live quietly with the consequences of her choices. And this would not have been easy for her because, several months after her servant returned, "Hagar bore Abram a son."[9]

Could it be that you, like Sarah, are also missing the obvious? Have you lashed out and wounded someone who wounded you? It may be something that seems much less than what the other person did to you. And maybe it actually is. But don't overlook it. Maybe that's why God has allowed the consequences to come back into your life.

If you and I really want the wounds within to heal, then we need to be brutally honest with ourselves. We need to stop focusing on *them* and ask God to open our eyes to our own faults. We need to have the courage to truly look at ourselves, as painful as it may be. Then *turn around.* Leave behind any pride ... rebellion ... rationalization ... excuses ... self-defense ... and self-pity. Turning around is a courageous choice — it's hard to do! It can hurt to take the plank out of your own eye, confront the past, change your focus, die to your pride, admit your wrong, deny your vengeance, face the person, risk another wound. And it takes courage to say you're sorry — sorry for your own planks and pride, shortcomings and sin, faults and failures — while leaving the other person to God. Yet, I can almost hear the applause in heaven as those who have gone before encourage and challenge you and me: "Repent, then, and turn to God, so that your sins may be wiped out, that times of refreshing may come from the Lord."[10]

The time for refreshing has come, but you and I must be willing to open our eyes. Then turn around. *Turn around!*

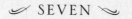

SEVEN

Wounding Hurts

*Doing the Right Thing Can Be
Painful to the Wounder*

Now the LORD was gracious to Sarah as he had said, and the LORD did for Sarah what he had promised. Sarah became pregnant and bore a son to Abraham in his old age, at the very time God had promised him. Abraham gave the name Isaac to the son Sarah bore him. When his son Isaac was eight days old, Abraham circumcised him, as God commanded him. Abraham was a hundred years old when his son Isaac was born to him.

Sarah said, "God has brought me laughter, and everyone who hears about this will laugh with me." And she added, "Who would have said to Abraham that Sarah would nurse children? Yet I have borne him a son in his old age."

The child grew and was weaned, and on the day Isaac was weaned Abraham held a great feast. But Sarah saw that the son whom Hagar the Egyptian had borne to Abraham was mocking, and she said to Abraham, "Get rid of that slave woman and her son, for that slave woman's son will never share in the inheritance with my son Isaac."

The matter distressed Abraham greatly because it concerned his son. But God said to him, "Do not be so distressed about the boy and your maidservant. Listen to whatever Sarah tells you, because it is through Isaac that your offspring will be reckoned. I will make the son of the maidservant into a nation also, because he is your offspring."

Early the next morning Abraham took some food and a skin of water and gave them to Hagar. He set them on her shoulders and then sent her off with the boy.

Genesis 21:1 – 14

As I was driving down the road one day recently, I noticed a gardener pruning a tree. I knew that the type of tree he was pruning required cutting out old branches to make room for the new growth. The beautiful summer flowers the tree is known for will not blossom on old limbs. Then God seemed to whisper in my ear, gently reminding me of the Heavenly Gardener who lovingly prunes the branches attached to the Vine.

Fruit on a vine is only borne in abundance on tender, new growth. As the wood of a branch gets older, it tends to harden. So even though a branch may be alive and connected to the vine, it can still fail to produce fruit. While leaving the branch connected to the vine, a gardener cuts back the old, hard wood, forcing the vine into new growth that will produce fruit instead of just leaves. In fact, there are times when a gardener cuts back the branch so drastically that all that is left is the nub where it is connected to the vine. As I drove by the gardener pruning the tree, it occurred to me that his pruning could be described as *wounding*.

Later, I went back and reread the illustration of a vine that Jesus used to describe our relationship to Him: "I am the true vine, and my Father is the gardener. He cuts off every branch in me that bears no fruit, while every branch that does bear fruit he prunes so that it will be even more fruitful."[1] He was describing the intentional wounding that results from God's pruning in a believer's life.

Does it hurt the Gardener to cut back the branch so far? I believe it does. But the writer to the Hebrews offers a key insight when he states, "No discipline [wounding or pruning] seems pleasant at the time, but painful. Later on, however, it produces a harvest of righteousness and peace for those who have been trained by it."[2] My guess is that the hurting heart of the Divine Wounder must surely be soothed when the result is abundant blessing and fruit.

Abraham was a wounder. When God initially called him to leave Ur of the Chaldeans, he obediently left everything behind in order to pursue God. In the beginning, one of his primary reasons for living a life of faith was God's promise of a son and descendants more numerous than stars in the sky.[3] Abraham may have been intrigued at the prospect of millions upon millions of descendants, but all he really wanted was one son to call his own. One baby he could hold. One boy he could talk to and teach, play with and enjoy, give things to and love. One son to whom he could leave everything. Just one descendant would be enough.

Hagar gave Abraham one descendant. His name was Ishmael. For fourteen years he was Abraham's only son. It doesn't require much imagination to know that Abraham, a very wealthy man whose holdings rivaled that of a small nation, lavished everything on Ishmael. He must have spent hours talking to Ishmael, playing with him, teaching him about managing a large household, and instructing him in sound business practices. Abraham loved Ishmael! And because God was central to his life, Abraham surely told Ishmael about the One who had leaned out of heaven to speak into his life when he had been living in Ur of the Chaldeans. The One who had promised to bless him and make him a channel of blessing to the world. The One who had called Abraham to a life of obedient faith; the One who had appeared to him again and again when he built his altars; the One who had spoken to him, comforted him, and delivered him from danger. I expect that Abraham confided to Ishmael that he, his firstborn, was the fulfillment of God's promise to bless him with descendants as numerous as the stars. Abraham surely grew increasingly attached to the boy as he wrapped years of longing around Hagar's son.

For fourteen years, Ishmael lived as a virtual prince, the beloved only son of a wealthy, powerful, well-known, and well-respected man. Rather than being humbly grateful for his privileges, however, Ishmael seemed to have inherited his mother's arrogance. It may not have been readily apparent when he was young and unchallenged in his position, but it became blazingly obvious when Sarah miraculously conceived and gave birth to her own son — at the age of ninety! Ishmael's world was rocked. No longer the sole focus of his father's attention and love, Ishmael nursed his wounds and patiently bided his time. Then he hit back. Hard.

On the day Sarah and Abraham's miracle son, Isaac, was weaned, Abraham threw a great feast to celebrate. Ishmael chose that moment to take revenge on the little boy who had dared to upset his world. While we don't know the exact form of the attack, we know it was brutal and likely focused on God's unique plan for Isaac's life, because the New Testament describes it as "persecution."[4]

One can only imagine the damage Ishmael's bullying would have done to his younger sibling had it remained a dirty little secret. It no doubt would have developed into a pattern of abusive behavior, perhaps even becoming life-threatening to Isaac. And it certainly would have been emotionally, spiritually, and psychologically damaging to the development of a little guy who was destined for a unique role in God's great plan of redemption.

But the persecution did not remain a secret for long, because Sarah caught Ishmael persecuting her boy. For years she had lived in silent acquiescence, patiently enduring the daily presence of Hagar and Ishmael. Now she broke her silence with the mother-of-all temper tantrums. Erupting in an explosion of pent-up rage, she let loose, wrapping her fury in righteous indignation and a mother's protective instincts for her child. In a tone that surely allowed no room for disagreement, she demanded that Abraham throw both Hagar and Ishmael out of the house: "Get rid of that slave woman and her son, for that slave woman's son will never share in the inheritance with my son Isaac."[5] The issue was laid out in harsh reality under the glaring spotlight of truth — because Hagar's son, Ishmael, was not the son God had promised to give Abraham. He was not heir to the promised spiritual birthright, which was Abraham's most valuable treasure.

Ishmael had been born as a result of Abraham's self-effort and in accordance with Abraham's self-will. When Abraham had grown impatient waiting for God to fulfill His promise of a son, Abraham had taken matters into his own hands. At eighty-five, Abraham had known he was running out of time to have children and perhaps thought God had forgotten His promise. So Abraham had run ahead of God. He had ignored God's principles for marriage,[6] in essence committed adultery, impregnated his servant, then hoped that God would retroactively bless everything. Even before Sarah had pronounced judgment, Abraham must have known deep in his heart that one day the rubber would finally hit the road. Now he could no longer keep hoping or pretending that everything was all right. It was impossible for both boys to have the same inheritance. They couldn't even live peaceably in the same home. The axe must finally fall. It was time for the Gardener's shears.

Wounds have a way of festering, don't they? Hagar, Sarah, Abraham, and now Ishmael and Isaac were all wounded. And wounds don't really self-heal. They seem to lie dormant, and then at an unsuspected moment, in an unexpected way, they erupt.

What wounds have been festering in your heart and life? Perhaps they've been lying dormant but now are beginning to surface, and you realize you are still hurting.

Sometimes our wounds, like Abraham's, are self-inflicted. They are the result of choices we have made according to our own self-effort and self-will. According to what we want. According to what we were convinced we had to have to be happy and fulfilled.

If we are honest, I expect all of us would admit to running full speed ahead at some point in our lives, praying for God to bless whatever it was that we were doing — or bless that relationship or bless that decision — all the while pretending, even to ourselves, that everything was okay and that God would let us get by with it. But deep down we know better. We have an uneasy feeling that this isn't right. Our conscience is warning us that we have run ahead of God and seized something for ourselves that we wanted. Maybe even something we believed God wanted to give us. We have felt we just couldn't wait one more day for God to keep His promise, whatever it was. With time seemingly running out, we may have jumped into a marriage, a career, a ministry, a pregnancy, an adoption, a business contract, or a second job.

So instead of waiting on God's time and for Him to give it to us in His way, we get it for ourselves. As a result, whatever we jumped into never works out like we had hoped. Actually, we can make a royal mess, as Abraham did.

If Abraham had been suppressing an uneasy feeling deep down in his spirit, it now erupted violently to the surface. His face must have turned white, then a deep red as he faced up to the fact that Sarah was right. This contrived arrangement was a mistake and not at all what God wanted. The shards of his shattered heart are evident in this poignant phrase from Scripture, "The matter distressed Abraham greatly because it concerned his son."[7] Although Isaac was the adored miracle child and the fulfillment of God's promise, Ishmael had been Abraham's beloved only child for fourteen years. How could throwing Ishmael out of the house be the right solution? And even if it was, how could he possibly do such a thing? *He loved Ishmael!*

As Abraham's love for Isaac, Ishmael, and Sarah all collided in an epic conflict of interests, he must have agonized over what to do. The turmoil in his home and in his heart surely paralyzed him, because God Himself leaned out of heaven to shake things loose. God first reassured Abraham and then told him exactly what to do: "Do not be so distressed about the boy and your maidservant. Listen to whatever Sarah tells you, because it is through Isaac that your offspring will be reckoned. I will make the son of your maidservant into a nation also, because he is your offspring."[8]

As stunningly incompatible as it seems with our human understanding of justice, God Himself, the Divine Gardener, confirmed that removing Hagar and Ishmael from Abraham's home was exactly the right thing to do. What Abraham might otherwise have disregarded as Sarah's irrational overreaction to Hagar and Ishmael was actually wise and godly counsel. It would protect Isaac, who no doubt would have been emotionally devastated and spiritually destroyed had he been left to the mercy of an antagonistic, arrogant, jealous older brother. And it would release Ishmael, already a young man, to discover and fulfill God's unique purpose for his life.

Once God clearly made His will known, Abraham exhibited no procrastination or hesitation in obeying. He could have resisted God's directive, complaining that, at nearly 105 years of age, he was much too old for a confrontation like this. But he didn't. Though it was surely the hardest thing Abraham had ever done, at this point in his life he did exactly what God had asked of him: "Early the next morning Abraham took some food and a skin of water and gave them to Hagar. He set them on her shoulders and then sent her off with the boy."[9]

I wonder what this moment must have been like for Hagar and Ishmael. I believe it's no exaggeration to say they were wounded to the extreme. By Abraham — a man of God and the friend of God! And here is the kicker: *it was the right thing to do.* But we also know that it wasn't just hard on Hagar and Ishmael; it was also hard on Abraham. Sometimes doing the right thing wounds others — and also wounds the wounder.

Are you having a difficult time accepting the fact that God can command us to do something that will hurt someone else? But sometimes He does. God's ways are not our ways and His thoughts are not our thoughts.[10] There are times He leads us in paths that go against conventional wisdom and the advice of those we might otherwise consider experts. He may direct us to make decisions that go against our own strongly held opinions or feelings. But when we choose to do what Abraham did — simply trust and obey — in time, we will discover that God always leads us on the right path.[11] Pruning produces a healthier, more vigorous, and more fruitful vine.

Sometimes obeying God carries collateral damage. I recall experiencing this myself when I taught Bible Study Fellowship in my city for twelve years. The class consistently maintained an active membership of five hundred women and approximately two hundred small children. Using the example Jesus set when He trained twelve disciples and then in turn used them to reach the world, I poured myself into the training of over seventy leaders who then were responsible for discipling a smaller group of either women or children entrusted to their care so that each class member, whether young or old, received individual attention and shepherding.

The leaders and I became like sisters. We grew together in our knowledge of the Scripture, our love for Jesus, and our desire to get others into God's Word. I truly loved those women. To this day, when I encounter one of them in a restaurant or at a meeting, the strong bond that was developed through our frequent interactions is still there. I feel the joy of the Shepherd when I hear that they are now teaching their own Bible classes, or serving in significant ways within their own churches, or writing Bible lessons for children, or organizing evangelistic outreaches. Some have gone on to write books. Some have written curriculum for other Bible studies.

Because the health and spiritual well-being of the entire class was my ultimate responsibility, I worked tirelessly to make sure that each leader was growing spiritually, was vibrant in her own faith and relationship with the Lord, and was fully engaged in discipling those she was responsible for. And I was ever mindful that I could not lead others farther than where I was myself, so I was constantly motivated to grow spiritually.

Because our class was the first such class in our area, the women who made up the leadership were good, churched women, but very few had deep roots to their faith. Very few had ever been in a Bible study before becoming a member. Their freshness, their lack of preconceived ideas about the Scripture, their eagerness to learn, their teachability made my role a delight. Truly a privilege.

So I don't want to tarnish the beautiful reflection of Him that I saw in my leaders' circle, but on a handful of occasions during those twelve years, a few of them stumbled. Badly. One confessed to me that she was struggling in her marriage, and as I looked into her eyes, I knew she was involved with someone else. She was. Another leader was unable to fulfill her role but lied to cover up her failure. When I confronted her, she tried to defend herself to me by lying again. Another leader was revealed to be a secret alcoholic.

At those times, I was confronted with a choice. I could compromise the holiness and righteousness that I believe God requires of His leaders and put my love for the leader, as well as my concern for her feelings, before the well-being of the entire class. Or I could remove her. I knew if I didn't take drastic action, the entire leadership would be infected, which would in turn infect the overall class. Quietly, lovingly, carefully so that few people, even within the leaders' circle, knew why the leader was no longer present, I removed each of them by asking them individually for their resignations. But in each case the offending leader was deeply hurt. Even though she knew her removal was justified, she was still wounded. By me. My heart was broken. I grieved for her and for myself and for the other leaders and for her class. Even though removing each one from leadership was the right thing to do, it hurt.

The only reason I would ever wound others whom I love and work with is because I love and trust God more, and He said so. And the only reason Abraham wounded Hagar and his beloved Ishmael was because he loved and trusted God more, and God said so. In each case, someone was wounded because God said so.

Does it surprise you that God sometimes commands us to do things He knows will result in others being wounded? You and I can delude ourselves into secretly hoping that a loving God will overlook the wrong that we, or others, have done if righting that wrong means wounding someone. We can falsely believe that a loving God will protect those He truly loves from this kind of hurt. We can buy into a prosperity message that convinces us that God's desire for us is to live pain-free, carefree, happy lives.

Sometimes our view of God seems to be the same view we have of a genie. We think that if we rub Him the right way with prayer and faith, He will pop up and give us what we want. It's a view that is drastically wrong. God's purpose for us is not to make us healthy, happy, prosperous, and problem-free. His ultimate purpose is to conform us to the image of His own dear Son, that we might bear much fruit to His glory.[12] And sometimes, in fulfilling that purpose, He allows us to be hurt.

There are times when the Divine Gardener cuts everything out of our lives except our relationship with Jesus. This kind of wounding not only hurts God, but hurts us as well. Maybe you haven't recognized it as pruning because it was an illness that landed you on a hospital bed, a termination from your job, a removal from your church position, a collapse of your business, a rejection by your peers, a dream that hit a dead end, a calling-out or a dressing-down.

Whatever it was or is, the wounds of divine pruning force us to pay attention to our relationship with God because He's all we have. And in the process, He strengthens our connection to the Vine, softens our hearts, and delights in our growth as our lives produce a greater harvest of spiritual fruit.

When have you been cut back to the nub? How did you respond

to the pain of the wound? I wonder ... how much more fruit would you and I produce if we were totally submissive to His wounding? If we embraced it instead of fighting it ...

Because your purpose and mine is to bring glory to God, fruit-bearing is not an option. We must bear fruit. And like a grapevine, in order to be fruitful we must submit to pruning. When we resist and fight back, what we are really doing is refusing to glorify God, thereby thwarting the very purpose for our existence.

We can trust the Gardener to use the shears in our lives skillfully, lovingly, and effectively. Trust Him. He's been pruning for years. He knows what He's doing.

We can also take comfort in knowing that Jesus Himself submitted to divine wounding. God the Father not only allowed but destined His Son to be wounded for a greater glory. Long before Jesus walked the earth, the prophet Isaiah described the Messiah as a suffering servant:

> Surely he took up our infirmities
>   and carried our sorrows,
> yet we considered him stricken by God,
>   smitten by him, and afflicted.
> But he was pierced for our transgressions,
>   he was crushed for our iniquities:
> the punishment that brought us peace was upon him,
>   and by his wounds we are healed....
> Yet it was the LORD's will to crush him and cause him
>   to suffer.[13]

It was the Lord's will to crush Him and cause Him to suffer? *How is that possible?* Who will ever fathom the love of a God who intentionally wounded His Son so that you and I might be healed of our own wounds! Surely the Father's great heart was broken; surely tears were flooding down the divine countenance; surely there were sobs choking the voice that had thundered from Mount Sinai — even as "he gave his one and only Son" to die on the cross so that "whoever believes in him shall not perish but have eternal life."[14]

Jesus, the Son of God, "did not retaliate; when he suffered, he made no threats. Instead, he entrusted himself to him who judges justly. Jesus Christ laid down his life for us."[15] Because He loves you and me. As a result, He bore much fruit. He ...

defeated the devil,

conquered the grave,

atoned for sin,

redeemed sinners,

opened heaven,

and triumphantly brought many sons and daughters to glory![16] Following His death on the cross, the Son of Man rose up from the dead[17] and returned to heaven to claim all of His former glory as the Son of God.[18] He now sits at the Father's right hand, with all authority in the universe placed under His feet.[19] No wonder the writer to the Hebrews exhorts us to, "Fix our eyes on Jesus, the author and perfecter of our faith, who for the joy set before him endured the cross, scorning its shame, and sat down at the right hand of the throne of God. Consider him who endured such opposition from sinful men, so that you will not grow weary and lose heart."[20]

Praise God that Jesus embraced the pain of divine wounding for the glory that would follow. He never confused *Him* with *them*.

I cannot comprehend such love for a wretched sinner like myself. But I can worship the One who loved me so much He wounded His own Son that by those very wounds I might be cleansed, forgiven, and healed. I can submit myself to the beloved Son who Himself submitted to God's wounding. And I can obey God's directives even when that obedience hurts someone else ... and me.

EIGHT

Rejected by Them

But Not by Him

She went on her way ...
Genesis 21:14

At the beginning of this book, I shared with you the experience my husband and I had when we were rejected by our church. What I didn't say was that the wound was intensified because it was piled on top of fresh, hurtful memories of previous rejection. A few months before my husband was voted out of his leadership position to the applause of the congregation, the board of deacons in that same church had voted to close the doors to the Bible class I had taught there for nine years. The reason? We used the Bible as our only textbook. This put my class of five hundred women in the crosshairs of the political and denominational tug-of-war that the church was caught up in. But God intervened on behalf of the Bible class — within a week of the deacons' vote, another wonderful church of the same denomination opened its doors to us, so that we never missed a class. Even so, because the church that had rejected my class was my own church, I felt the need to respond in some way. But how? What could I do or say in response to such intentional rejection? I didn't know. But I knew God did, and so I cried out to Him, opening my ears to what He would say as I listened with my eyes on the pages of my Bible.

At the time, I was studying Jeremiah in my personal devotions. I was impressed that God often told Jeremiah to act out his prophetic messages. As I applied the Scripture to my situation, I wondered how I might act out a message of love to the church that had closed its doors to my Bible class. I didn't know how to do that, so I simply prayed, *God, how do I do that? What would You have me to do? What is the message You would have me act out?*

I was reminded that I had been raised in a denomination that practiced a form of baptism my present church did not recognize — which meant the baptism I had experienced as a young girl was not recognized by the leaders of the church I was now attending. The thought came to me that I could act out God's message of love by offering to submit to the form of baptism accepted and practiced by my present church. From God's perspective, I knew I didn't need to be rebaptized. But I wanted to honor God and identify with the people He loved, and I felt one way to do that was to submit myself to baptism by immersion.

So at the age of thirty-seven, after thirty years of living out a committed Christian life, I followed through on what I believed to be God's leading. On a Sunday evening shortly after my class had been voted out, with my father in the waters beside me and my husband and three children in the pews in front of me, I was baptized by immersion as a demonstration of loving identification with the church that had rejected my class.

While I did not expect the church deacons to reverse their decision, I did think the church members would be disarmed by my action and receive me and my gesture kindly. Instead of being kindly received, however, I was shunned. In the weeks that followed, people turned away from me as I walked down the halls and avoided me when I entered the classrooms. Rather than softening hearts, what I intended as an act of love had actually hardened them.

While I don't know why I was shunned, there may be two explanations. Either they did not understand my gesture of love even though I had written a public letter giving the reason for my decision to be rebaptized. Or perhaps my gesture had made them feel guilty for their rejection of my husband. Maybe I had embarrassed the congregation. Maybe instead of apologizing, they simply turned their backs, hoping both of us would go away. Which we did. While many good friends stood by us and stood up for us, we knew that we had obviously become a problem for the majority. So taking great care not to split the church by forcing people to take sides, we quietly left.

But the wound of their rejection hurt. Later I found comfort as I related to the rest of Jeremiah's testimony:

> My eyes fail from weeping,
>   I am in torment within;
> my heart is poured out on the ground....
> I remember my affliction ...
>   the bitterness and the gall.
> I well remember them,
>   and my soul is downcast within me.
> Yet this I call to mind
>   and therefore I have hope:
>
> Because of the LORD's great love we are not consumed,
>   for his compassions never fail.
> They are new every morning;
>   great is your faithfulness.[1]

Jeremiah obeyed God's instructions to act out God's Word, but his actions were not well received either. In the end, his heart was broken, and his life was taken by God's people who stoned him to death. *Wounded!* But Jeremiah was obedient, even unto death. His trust in God and his testimony of God's faithfulness still reverberate over twenty-five hundred years later. Not only are the words of his testimony the basis for a beloved hymn sung in churches all over the world today, "Great Is Thy Faithfulness," but that hymn was the very one that our family sang to my mother as she left this world and entered into her heavenly Home.

As hurt as I was by the church's rejection, my relationship with God was strong enough and my understanding of His Word thorough enough to know that being rejected by the church did not mean being rejected by Him. As we walked away from the church that had been our home for over fifteen years, I had the overwhelming awareness that God walked with us. Our tears were on His face, and He bore our shame and disgrace too. God understands how it feels to be rejected by His own people.[2]

As Hagar walked away from the home she had known for over twenty-four years, painful memories from long ago must have resurfaced in her mind. Cries and confusion, frustrations and fears, anger and agony, turmoil and tears — all long forgotten — must have come back in a rush. Did she flash back to a day twenty years earlier when she had fled into that same desert? Now it seemed to be happening all over again! Did Hagar choke on her sobs, her breath coming in ragged gasps, as she relived the painful memories of her past? It just wasn't fair! *Where was God?*

Did her flashbacks also include memories of God's presence? Did she remember that God had been right there with her on the desert road leading to the wilderness? Hadn't He put His arms of love around her and held her close to reassure her and quiet her sobs? But ... *where was He now?* How could this be happening to her — *again* — after all these years? She had repented! She had turned back and submitted to Sarah. She and Sarah had seemed to work out a cordial relationship. How had everything disintegrated so suddenly?

Once again, Hagar found herself on the desert road — and this time it was not her choice. She'd been given no opportunity to explain herself or to have Ishmael apologize and try to make amends. She had been given no chance at all to defend herself or her son or to even discuss the situation. She had just been thrown out of the family! And once again, she must have cried out in her heart, *God, where are You? Where is the One Who Sees me? Are You looking the other way and are somehow missing what is happening here? Do You see but not care anymore? Do You see and care, but You're somehow helpless to intervene ... sacrificing me and my son for some greater purpose? God, are You on their side?*

At this point, Hagar could have tossed her head, lifted her chin, and emphatically decided, "No, God is not on their side. The God I know would never have told Abraham to do such a thing. Their God is not God. My God is God." And she could have begun to worship a god she made up — a god that suited her by accommodating her point of view.

I can't help but wonder ... how many churches, and even denominations, have divided because of a similar attitude? Two factions disagreeing, with each side claiming God is on their side. In Hagar's case, she was honest enough to see and accept the obvious — God had agreed with Sarah. He *was* on their side!

As Hagar trudged down the dusty wilderness road with the water jug slung over her slumped shoulder, a parcel of food clutched in her hand, and her young son by her side, I imagine she stumbled. Her vision blurred. Her gait weaved in a meandering, mindless forward motion, not knowing where to go, just knowing she had to get out of *there*.

Surely all she could think was, *God agreed with Sarah. God instructed Abraham to throw me out!* The consternation must have been overwhelming. It no doubt clouded her thinking, dismantled her faith, and left her feeling utterly abandoned. Had she just been rejected, not only by God's people, *but by God?*

Perhaps you have had similar thoughts that led you to a similar conclusion — that if God has allowed you or those you care about to be treated in such an ungodly way by those who identify with Him, then you want no part of them — *or Him.*

One result of my Bible class being removed from our church, and then my husband's subsequent rejection from his leadership role, was that we heard from others who had had similar experiences. Our rejection seemed to stir up memories of their own painful woundings. One woman who had been an active Christian for most of her life wrote, "My most severe hurts and disappointments have come from Christian believers.... Wounds from Christian swords heal very slowly."

Wounds from a "Christian sword" heal slowly because they seem to hurt the worst and penetrate the deepest. Has your relationship with God been strong enough to carry you through the painful rejection? Have you hidden yourself in your Heavenly Father's embrace? Buried your head on His shoulder as He has soothed your hurt with words of comfort? Have you felt the compassion of Someone who knows firsthand what it's like to be rejected by His own people? Were you able to conclude that their rejection of you was really *their* problem and not yours?

Or do you find yourself feeling more like Hagar? In the face of rejection, her faith wilted and then evaporated, leaving her with what must have felt like incurable wounds. Hagar's relationship with God, though established years earlier when she first ran away, does not appear to have developed into one that could handle this type of rejection.

As you read Hagar's story, perhaps you are reflecting on your own … *If God truly cares about me, why don't I feel Him pursuing me? Where is He? Why don't I hear His voice inquiring, "What's the matter?" Where are His gentle instructions telling me what to do?* Maybe this is the very reason you are reading this book. Because God *is* pursuing you at this moment, coming to you through the story of Hagar. Don't let your own tears blind you or your own thoughts deafen you to an encounter with Him. Right here. Right now. You may have been rejected by them, *but you are not rejected by Him.*

 NINE

Wandering
in the Wilderness

God Is Still There

She went on her way and wandered
in the desert of Beersheba.

Genesis 21:14

A wilderness is defined as an uncultivated, uninhabited, inhospitable region. At least that's the definition I was given when I googled it. I would also describe a wilderness as dry, barren, lonely, and rocky. And it was in a spiritual wilderness that I found myself several years ago. Because it was a time in my life that was dry ... seemingly devoid of the rain of God's blessing; barren ... seemingly devoid of evidence of real fruit in my life; lonely ... devoid of any conscious awareness of God's presence; and it was rocky ... littered with problems and obstacles and hard things. If I could have pinpointed one particular trigger that launched me into my wilderness experience, it would have been my mother's departure for heaven. Not only did my grief leave me with a feeling of emptiness and deep sadness, but there were many circumstances around the time of her death that seemed to drive me into a spiritually dry, barren, lonely, rocky place. Life just seemed to close in on me.

One morning, I was especially conscious of the oppression and darkness that seemed to be crushing my spirit to the point that I found breathing difficult. I slipped into the place where I meet the Lord early in the morning, intending to open my Bible to the verses on which I had been meditating the day before. But as divine providence would have it, I made a "mistake." Instead of opening to the intended passage, I opened to a chapter that was several pages past where I had been. But before I could correct my mistake, my eye fell on this verse: "The people remained at a distance, while Moses approached the thick darkness where God was."[1] The verse seemed to be illuminated. It leaped up off the page as I heard God whispering to me through the words, *Anne, most people shy away from the wilderness. They don't like the darkness of oppression, loneliness, dryness, barrenness. They don't like to be in a hard place. If they think I'm going to lead them there, they resist, back off, and want no part of following Me. But, Anne, Moses approached the thick darkness. Because that's where I was. And that's where I still am, Anne. Embrace the darkness.*

Before I could answer Him, before I could even pray, almost before I could even think, I found myself turning several pages back to where I was "supposed" to have been reading. The first verse of that reading was, "While Aaron was speaking to the whole Israelite community, they looked toward the desert, and there was the glory of the LORD appearing in the cloud."[2] The desert is another name for the wilderness! That dry, barren, rocky, lonely place where I seemed to be. And I knew God was telling me, *Anne, I am here. Look closely. You will see My glory in the dark cloud.*

I was not consciously aware of seeing His glory at that moment. All I knew was that God had spoken to me and told me He was there. And so I bowed my head, with tears slipping down my face, and whispered to Him in response, *If You are truly in the darkness, then I embrace it. I want to be where You are.*

God is in the darkness and God is in the wilderness. I now know that by personal experience. But although Hagar had known God's presence in her wilderness years earlier, she had forgotten. She did not know that now. So when she suddenly found herself thrust not only into a dry, barren, lonely, rocky physical place, she also found herself in a spiritual wilderness — alone for the first time in thirty years and burdened with the responsibility of providing for the physical, emotional, intellectual, spiritual, and practical needs of a difficult teenage boy. Hagar desperately needed help. She knew she couldn't go back, but she had no idea how to go forward. And so she wandered ... through the desert of Beersheba[3] and the wastelands of her own spiritual and emotional devastation.

You don't necessarily have to be a single mother, thrust there by an untimely death or a nasty divorce, to find yourself in Hagar's situation. Like me, maybe life has just crashed in on you. Wounds and rejection can pile up. Perhaps you feel you have no one to turn to, no one to talk to, no one to help you. If you and I are not careful, that aloneness can cause us to wander in our spirits also. We want to get away from the darkness, to get out of the wilderness, but in our frantic effort we stumble from remorse to resentment, from self-pity to self-flagellation, from self-deception to depression, from brokenness to bitterness, from faith to agnosticism, from frustration to anger, from hurt to hardness, from hardness to helplessness. May I ask you something I have asked myself? Deep down in the hidden chambers of your soul, are you offended by God? Angry with Him even? Are you wandering *from* God? You thought you knew Him, but now He seems remote at best. The solemn conclusion I've come to is that if He is everywhere, that means He is also in the wilderness. And if I can't turn to Him there, who can I turn to?

As Hagar stumbled through the vast wilderness, her clothing catching on thorns, her feet stumbling over the rocks, her throat choking on the dust, she lost sight of everything but her own despair. Her self-preoccupation, though understandable, blinded her to God's presence and to God's provision. But God was not blind to Hagar. He was still there with her and watching her every step. While His gaze never left her, His heart must have ached over her helpless, hopeless condition. *Hagar, remember Me? I am still the One who sees you.*[4] *You're not alone. I'm right here.* But Hagar was so wrapped up in her wounds that she did not look up; she did not call on God; she did not pray. With her gaze cast down, all she could do was cry.

As the desert wind blew swirling dust in her face and the sky turned brazen from the heat, her mind must have snapped into panic mode, triggered by a feeling of total helplessness. She didn't know where she could go or where she could live or how she could support herself and her son. Up until the moment she had walked away from Abraham's household, Hagar had led a somewhat sheltered existence. She hadn't needed to give a thought to providing the food on her table or the clothes on her back or the roof over her head. Abraham had generously supplied everything she had ever needed. Now she was suddenly on her own, responsible for finding basic necessities for herself and for her son. She must have felt totally helpless, because, humanly speaking, she *was* totally helpless.

Hagar's overall realization of her completely helpless condition was pushed to the breaking point, not only by her wandering in the wilderness, but by her very real, immediate physical needs. She was desperate for water for herself and for Ishmael: "When the water in the skin was gone, she put the boy under one of the bushes."[5] Neither of them would survive much longer without water. There was almost no chance she would ever find it on her own. And it may be that it wasn't just her body that was dehydrated, but it was her spirit that was parched because she felt utterly separated from God.

I know what it's like to be spiritually parched and desperately dry. Thirsty for Him. Thirsty for the same One who has revealed Himself in the past to His children in the wilderness. As I have pondered the revelation that God's glory could be seen in the desert place ... in the wilderness ... I have asked Him to show me. Thousands of years before, Moses had made a similar request, so I have reasoned, why couldn't I?

So one morning, I opened my Bible and turned to Exodus 33 and 34, the account of Moses' request for God to reveal His glory and God's answer.[6] I read that God had put Moses in the cleft of a rock, covered him with His hand, then removed His hand and allowed Moses to gaze, not on His face, but on the "backside" of His glory.

As I pondered this passage, I understood that God's glory is not just a golden, shining light or cloud. His glory is His character.[7] And then God began to "speak" to me ... phrase by phrase ... *Anne, I have put you in the cleft of a rock. I have intentionally put you in a hard place. You are stuck there. But I have covered you with My hand, and you have felt the nearness of My presence. Then I removed My hand so that you have felt abandoned by Me. But Anne, look back. Look back! My glory can be seen if you will look back.*

So I opened the eyes of my heart and mind. I looked back on my life and some of my more recent experiences. *That's when I saw His glory ...*

- When I was asked to give my testimony to an arena gathering of twenty thousand people ten days after my mother went to heaven, God kept my knees from buckling, my voice from quavering, my tears from falling ... then gave me His words to offer the hope of heaven to those who were there. As I look back, I can see His comfort that He had given me was enough to share so that I could comfort others.[8]

- When I had radical personnel changes in my ministry that could have caused major damage to my small team, He rallied the core staff around me, then brought in other outstanding personnel so that today we are stronger and better than we were before we faced the changes. As I look back, I can see His wisdom that perfected our operations.[9]

- When I underwent major abdominal surgery, He surrounded me with love, provided for my every need, and blessed me with the 24/7 attentiveness of my two daughters. Then He gave me His strength four weeks later to climb up on a platform surrounded by eight thousand women and deliver three messages, lead one workshop, and oversee the simulcast for our *Just Give Me Jesus* revival in Augusta, Georgia. As I look back, I can see His strength that was more than sufficient in my weakness.[10]

- When my husband, Danny, was rushed to the hospital where he remained for three weeks with a MRSA infection, it was at a time when my schedule "happened" to be clear so that I only had to cancel one commitment to be with him. And God answered prayer by miraculously bringing Danny back from the brink of death with a spiritually revived heart! As I look back, I can see that not only is He Jehovah-Rophe, the One Who Heals us, but He also is the Good Shepherd who goes before us, leads us, and cares for us as we follow Him.[11]

I actually could go on for pages, sharing example after example, glimpse on top of glimpse of His glory that He has given me in the darkness. The interesting thing I have learned is that I can't seem to see His glory at the moment of my distress. As He told Moses, I have not been allowed to see His "face" ... the front side. I can't seem to see in advance how He is going to provide, undergird, equip, sustain, strengthen, or bless me when life closes in around me. But when He brings me through, I look back and I can see that He has been with me every moment, every step of the way.

So ... if you find yourself stuck in the cleft of a rock, would you ask the God of Moses to show you His glory? Then look back ...

And if you are wandering in the wilderness — that spiritually dry, barren, lonely, rocky place — would you remember that the God of Hagar is still there?

TEN

God Stands By

*He Hears Your Cry
for Help*

When the water in the skin was gone, she put the boy under one of the bushes. Then she went off and sat down nearby, about a bowshot away, for she thought, "I cannot watch the boy die." And as she sat there nearby, she began to sob.

Genesis 21:15 – 16

God doesn't always reveal Himself to us as dramatically as we would like Him to. Nor does God always answer our cry immediately. But when we call on Him, He hears. And He will answer. I have experienced His faithfulness to stand by and answer when I call.

Four weeks following major surgery I led our *Just Give Me Jesus* revival, as I mentioned in the previous chapter. The week's schedule included team meetings, a press conference, individual media interviews, and a videotaping, as well as my own preparation. It was then capped off by the revival itself, which was held in the James Brown Arena Friday evening and all day Saturday. When I stepped up on the platform Friday night, although I should have been weak and exhausted after such an intense week, I don't think I've ever felt stronger or more confident that God was going to see me through to the end.

God poured out His blessing that Friday night as we witnessed hundreds coming to the cross in repentance of sin. And because He doesn't run out of blessings, He also poured them out in abundance all day Saturday, which was a ministry marathon. He gave me energy to give the opening devotional, the first message, the interactive Bible study workshop, and the final message.

About halfway through the last message, I felt led to share about my surgery with the audience. I knew that I had experienced a continuous and miraculous infusion of His strength and power throughout the weekend in particular, and I wanted those present to be encouraged in their own journeys of faith by glimpsing His glory. So in just a sentence or two, I briefly shared what I had been through, asking them, *If He can help me, then why do you think He can't help you also?*

Almost as soon as the words went out of my mouth, I began to feel weak and dizzy. I placed my hands on the cross-shaped podium to balance and steady myself, but as my tongue thickened and my words became slurred, I knew I was going to go down. Inside, my thoughts were somewhat frantic. I had just told the audience that the Spirit of God had given me strength and was available to do so for them. If I went down, it would communicate to them that I was a liar, and so was He. My collapse would say without words that He could not be depended on in an impossible, or even difficult, situation. I knew it would tarnish His glory that I so earnestly had wanted them to see. Only a few moments had passed, I'm sure, but it was enough time for me to become clammy and damp, and for my eyes to begin to lose their focus as the arena around me blurred. Silently, in my heart, I cried out! The prayer was very simple. *Jesus, help me!*

At the moment I cried out, a cool breeze swept across the platform ... and kept blowing. I regained my composure as my body felt refreshed by the moving air. I stopped slurring and my focus returned. My words began to come out clearly, and as I closed with a challenge to live for Jesus, then gave the benediction, my voice was actually dynamic and forceful.

The next day, I asked our production manager if he or any of the people behind the cameras had noticed me struggling and turned on a fan. He laughed when he said, *Anne, there is no fan in that older venue that we could have turned on even if we had wanted to. And*

I knew God had heard my cry and intervened to save me from a dramatic collapse.

God stands by. And not just on a public-arena platform, but He stands by in life. Every moment of every day in every situation. But you and I may need to cry out before He helps us. How disheartening it would be if one day we get to heaven and discover all the situations we may have been saved from, all the blessings we may have experienced, if we had only cried out to Him for help but didn't.

A family friend related to me that for years he had shared the gospel with his beloved doctor. Because of serious health issues that required my friend to make repeated office visits, he and the doctor had become close friends. The doctor, who was of another religion, rejected again and again the Good News that my friend presented to him. But one night a tremendous earthquake shook the entire area where they both lived.

Several days later, my friend was once again in the doctor's office. This time, the doctor had a warm smile on his face and a sparkle in his eyes as he shared that he had finally repented of his sin and trusted Jesus as his Savior. My friend was thrilled! When he asked how the doctor had finally come to that decision after resisting it for so long, the doctor replied, "I was born again between the bed and the floor." Then with a smile he explained that the earthquake had thrown him out of his bed and that before he hit the floor he had cried out to be saved from his sin. And God, who had been standing by, saved him.

The Bible portrays Abraham as a man who knew what it was to cry out to God. His prayer life was one of his strengths. He often talked with God not only on his own behalf, but also on behalf of others.[1] When he built his altars for prayer, he did so in plain, public view.[2] There is no doubt that Hagar had witnessed Abraham building those places of prayer, as well as overheard him talking to God. So it is especially curious why Hagar, after twenty-five years of living in Abraham's household, didn't follow his example and pray about her desperate situation.

Maybe Hagar was so overwhelmed by a combination of emotional and physical trauma — shock, fear, confusion, thirst, and exhaustion — that it never occurred to her to pray. Or perhaps it did occur to her, but maybe she thought of God as someone who was available at altars and for spiritual needs but not in the desert and for practical needs — like water and directions. Maybe she reasoned God didn't really care about her anyway, at least not as a distinct individual in her own right. Perhaps the only reason He really cared about her in the first place was because she was a member of Abraham's household. If so, she must have felt she had now forever lost God's blessing and forfeited His attention. Even if she once felt assured that He at least cared about her son, that hope may have evaporated when Isaac was born. Or maybe she was just giving God the silent treatment, angry because He had not only allowed this horrible event to happen but seemed to have directed it.

Whatever the reason, Hagar did not pray. In fact, it's hard to detect any evidence of faith in her actions: "When the water in the skin was gone, she put the boy under one of the bushes. Then she went off and sat down nearby, about a bowshot away, for she thought, 'I cannot watch the boy die.'"[3] Die? *Die?* I want to say, *Hagar, snap out of it. You're feeling sorry for yourself again. Aren't you forgetting something? Something very important. Didn't God tell you He would increase your descendants?*[4] *Doesn't that imply that Ishmael will have children? Ishmael is not even married yet. Where is your faith, Hagar? Take your eyes off your circumstances and root your faith in God's character and in God's Word.* But Hagar didn't. Instead, she collapsed in despair.

Is that where you are, at the end of your rope? Have you thrown your wounded heart under a bush of bitterness or unforgiveness, self-pity or self-defense, regret or revenge, resentment or rationalization, fear or frustration? Don't let your anger harden your heart or cause you to blame God for what has happened. Don't let it prevent you from calling on God. Now.

I pray that the following story will encourage you to call out …

As a Muslim, Maria[5] considers herself to be one of Hagar's descendants. She found herself in a truly desperate situation, living with a husband who is a religious fanatic, and who beat her continually. Not only was she being abused, but her husband also abused their five-year-old son, beating him and burning him with cigarettes.

Maria prayed over and over to her god but received no answers. Finally, in sheer desperation, she cried out — *God, where are you? Who are you?* In her own words, this is what happened …

"I was weeping on the floor, crying out for help. All of a sudden, I saw a flash of bright light. It filled the room and was the most beautiful, calming, and assuring feeling I have ever had in my life. But then something even more remarkable happened — Jesus stood before me and spoke to me. His face was covered with shining sun, His hands reached out to me to invite me to His embrace, they were scarred from being pierced. He told me, 'I am here. You are not forgotten. I died for you. This evil will pass — I will deliver you from it.' Then He was gone. I have never felt so secure and loved in my life.

"I next met a believer who showed me from the Bible how to receive Jesus as my Savior and become His disciple. I was more than eager to commit my life to Him even though it might mean that I would be killed. It didn't matter — I never want to be away from my Jesus! I am a Jesus follower now."

The same Angel of the Lord who was standing by thousands of years ago for Hagar was standing by for Hagar's "daughter." And as thrilling as Maria's testimony is ... and as true ... it dramatically underscores the fact that the Angel of the Lord is standing by for you and me as well. God hears our cries of desperation, and He will answer. If only we had eyes to see into the invisible realm, we would see Him standing there in the light of His glory, with arms outstretched, eyes tear-filled, reassuring us of His presence and His love and His peace and His power to save.

In her misery, Hagar may have blamed everyone else for what had happened. Yet at this critical moment in her life, it really didn't matter anymore who was to blame for her hopeless and helpless circumstances. It didn't matter if it was Pharaoh's fault for giving her to Abraham and Sarah, or Abraham and Sarah's fault for taking her out of Egypt, or Sarah's fault for giving Hagar to Abraham, or Abraham's fault for sleeping with her, or her own fault for arrogantly despising Sarah, or Ishmael's fault for persecuting Isaac. There was enough blame to go around. The only thing that mattered now was that Hagar could not take any more of the desert, the heat, the thirst, the fear, the sound of Ishmael's cries. She could not take any more of the consequences. She had had it. But still, she did not look up.

Did she suffer from delusion? *Abraham is not an authentic man of faith. He is as wretched as any pagan back in Egypt.*

Did she claim self-defense? *If God had all the facts straight, He would be on my side.*

Did she indulge in self-pity? *What did I ever do to deserve this?*
Did she wallow in resentment? *Why should I be held responsible
    for Ishmael's behavior? Everybody knows teenagers do and say
    things they shouldn't.*
Did she experience remorse? *If only I had been a better mother
    and kept a closer eye on Ishmael, he wouldn't
    have gotten into trouble.*
Did she fear the worst? *Because of my sin and failure, will my
    child never have a future? Will he die in his lost condition
    because I can't find my way? Have I lost God's blessing
    and caused my son to miss His blessing too?*

I imagine Hagar in a posture of absolute grief and desperation
— hunched over with her head between her knees and her hands
wrapped over her head, sobbing, rocking back and forth on her
heels. Meanwhile, Ishmael, barely shaded under one of the few scrub
bushes that dotted the barren landscape, was literally dying of thirst.
Perhaps he had been so pampered and spoiled in Abraham's home
that he had never developed survival skills or learned to take the
initiative. So he curled up in what I assume was a hopeless fetal position, echoing his mother's helplessness and hopelessness, and cried
his eyes out. Because Hagar had lost her way, he seemed to be convinced that they were both going to die.

Yet looking on from heaven was One who was standing by. With
infinite tenderness and compassion, His eyes never left Hagar and
Ishmael. His ears were attentive, listening for the slightest cry for
His help. How long would they persist in their misery? How far
down would they have to go before they looked up? God seemed to
be patiently waiting to hear their call.

The Old Testament story of Jonah provides another dramatic

Biblical example of God's intervention when He was called. It took place approximately one thousand years after Hagar. Jonah was a prophet commanded by God to deliver a message to Nineveh, the capital city of Israel's worst enemy, Assyria. Instead of obeying, Jonah bought passage on a boat headed for Tarshish, which was in the exact opposite direction from where God had told him to go. *Jonah ran from God.* But as we have already seen in Hagar's life, that's impossible. No one can outrun God.

Almost as soon as Jonah set out to sea, a great storm arose. When the ship he was traveling on was swamped, he admitted to the sailors that he was running from his God. To save themselves and their ship, they threw him overboard. Here is where the story gets really interesting. Jonah ended up in the belly of a great fish, which swallowed him as soon as he hit the water. I can't even imagine what that must have been like! To find himself in the slimy jaws of a great fish, sucked in by a huge whirlpool that carried him like a tiny leaf on churning sea foam, surrounded by smaller fish and debris, and then to feel the compression of the fish's stomach as the gastric juices began to digest him! Surely, he had hit rock bottom. There was no place lower on the entire planet than the belly of that fish. But it was from those very depths that he finally looked up and cried out for God's help:

> In my distress I called to the LORD,
> > and he answered me.
> From the depths of the grave I called for help,
> > and you listened to my cry.
> You hurled me into the deep,
> > into the very heart of the seas,
> > and the currents swirled about me;

all your waves and breakers
    swept over me.
I said, "I have been banished
    from your sight;
yet I will look again
    toward your holy temple."
The engulfing waters threatened me,
    the deep surrounded me;
    seaweed was wrapped around my head.
To the roots of the mountains I sank down;
    the earth beneath barred me in forever.
But you brought my life up from the pit,
O LORD my God.

When my life was ebbing away,
    I remembered you, LORD,
and my prayer rose to you.[6]

Jonah had God's undivided attention. He was standing by when Jonah prayed. And He answered — immediately. He caused the fish literally to vomit Jonah onto dry land. God rescued Jonah, but He didn't release him from his divine assignment. God held firm to His original command, sending Jonah straight to Nineveh. And Jonah, newly recommitted to the will of God, went and preached. As a result, the entire city of Nineveh, from the king on down to the common people in the streets, repented of sin and submitted themselves to God.

One thousand years after Jonah, we see this dynamic still clearly at work in Jesus' relationship with his disciples. They were straining against the oars of their boat during a wind storm on the Sea of

Galilee. The Bible tells us that when Jesus walked toward them, "He was about to pass by them." He did not step into their boat and calm the sea until they cried out to Him.[7]

If God heard the cry of His disciples in the midst of a storm . . .

If God heard the cry of a disobedient, rebellious, defiant prophet who had sunk so low as to end up in the belly of a great fish . . .

If God heard the cry of a desperate Muslim mother . . .

If God heard the cry of my friend's doctor during the earthquake . . .

If God heard my cry at the podium on an arena platform . . .

Why do you think He will not hear your cry?

God is a gentleman. He won't force His way into your life, or insist on helping when you don't seem to want it, or even push Himself into your situation. He waits for you to *ask* before He intervenes. Almost four thousand years after Hagar, three thousand years after Jonah, two thousand years after the disciples, God is still standing by, dear reader. Yes, He is. But He may be waiting for your call. So call Him. Cry out, now. Use the words of my prayer. *Jesus, help me . . .*

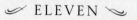

ELEVEN

The Silence Is Broken

God Is a Prayer-Hearing,
Prayer-Answering,
Miracle-Working God[1]

God heard the boy crying, and the angel of God called to Hagar from heaven ...

Genesis 21:17

Sometimes the most valuable lessons are caught, not taught. Like Abraham's example to Ishmael, the life my parents lived in our home provided some of my most important lessons.

One incident stands out with sparkling clarity . . .

The week following my seventeenth birthday, my father was the guest speaker at a public school assembly honoring my graduating high school class. The assembly was open to the families and friends of the graduates, and since my father was the speaker, it was held off-campus in a civic auditorium. I was behind schedule and ran out of the house, calling over my shoulder to let my parents know I was going on ahead of them since I had promised to pick up some friends on the way.

I jumped in Mother's little VW Beetle, which she had loaned to me for the occasion, floored the accelerator, and flew down the winding, one-lane mountain road that led up to our house. I made great time until I rounded one sharp curve and, to my horror, was confronted by a big Buick Riviera coming up the road. I slammed on the brakes, turned the wheel hard to the right, plowed into an embankment, but not before slamming into the front of the oncoming car.

With the sound of crunching metal, breaking glass, and spinning tires ringing in my ears, I tried to open my door, but it was smashed shut. So I crawled over the stick-shift and climbed out the passenger door. The Buick's driver was standing beside her car with eyes widened by shock and fear. I recognized her as a neighbor, Mrs. Pickering.

I quickly apologized, "I'm so sorry, Mrs. Pickering. It's all my fault. Please help me pull the fender off the tire and let me see if the car will start. I'm soooo late." She did as she was asked, and then I climbed back through the passenger door, crawled over the stick shift, and into the driver's seat. I backed the car down the embankment, rolled down the window on the passenger door, and pleaded, "Mrs. Pickering, please don't say anything to my daddy. I'll tell my parents after the service, but I don't want to say anything now."

I drove slowly through town to pick up my friends, but then something caught my eye. When I looked in the rearview mirror, I saw flashing blue lights. *Could this day get any worse?* I couldn't believe I was being pulled over by the local police! The tears began to flow. The officer walked up to the window and for a moment stared alternately at me and the car before finally stating the obvious: "Well, little lady, it looks like you've been in a wreck."

I nodded. He waited and stared some more.

"Make sure you drive more carefully," he finally said.

I nodded again, and he let me go.

By the time I picked up my friends, I was the wreck! They peppered me with questions that I tearfully tried to answer as we drove to the service. When we arrived, I carefully parked the car so the smashed side was hidden against some bushes, hoping no one would notice and ask my mother what had happened to her car. Then I ran to take my place in the line of seniors who were already marching into the auditorium.

I don't remember much about the service except that my father strode across the platform, looked straight at me, and then announced to one and all that I had never caused him any problems and had always been a joy to my mother and him. I wanted to die!

Following the service, I was trying to make a quick getaway when someone said, "Anne, your father wants to see you." I felt certain that judgment was about to fall. Instead, my father was simply responding to the request of photographers and reporters who wanted a picture of him adjusting the tassel on the mortarboard of his graduating senior. The next day, our picture was on the front page of Asheville's *Citizen-Times*. Clearly visible were the mascara streaks running down my face, which I'm sure readers attributed to my emotion over graduation!

Finally, I was able to slip away, return my friends to their respective houses, and drive back home. Very slowly. As I drove, I prayed, "Please, dear God, *please* have my daddy anywhere — he can be on the phone, he can be in his study, he can be taking a walk — just please don't have him where I will have to see him right now, because I have to think this through. I promise I'm going to tell him about the wreck — just not now."

I pulled up into the driveway, parked the car so the crushed side was shielded from the view of anyone in the house, then tiptoed up to the front door. I opened the screen door very carefully so it wouldn't squeak, slipped inside, and was poised to run up the stairs to my room when I glanced into the kitchen. There stood my father, his piercing blue eyes directed straight toward me.

I paused for what seemed a very long moment frozen in time. Then I ran to him and threw my arms around his neck. "Daddy, I'm so sorry. If you knew what I'd done, you never would have said all those nice things about me at the service." I told him about my wreck — how I'd driven way too fast and smashed into the neighbor's car. I told him it wasn't her fault; it was all mine. As I wept on his shoulder, he said four things that taught me important truths, not only about life, but also, ultimately, about my Heavenly Father:

- "Anne, I knew all along about your wreck. Mrs. Pickering came straight up the mountain and told me — I was just waiting for you to come tell me yourself."
- "I love you."
- "We can fix the car."
- "You are going to be a better driver because of this."[2]

What an example of grace! In the arms of my earthly father, I experienced love and forgiveness that I didn't deserve. And it gave me a deeper understanding of what it means to experience the loving, forgiving embrace of my Heavenly Father.

Sooner or later, all of us are involved in some kind of wreck — it might be physical, emotional, financial, or relational. The wreck may be your own fault or someone else's. When the damage is your fault, there's a good chance you'll be confronted by the flashing blue lights of the morality police. They'll gape at you and the debris and say, "My, my. It looks like you've been in a wreck. You've made a mess of your life, and you've hurt other people." As if you don't already know you'd been in a wreck! Their criticism isn't helpful; it just deepens the hurt and shame and guilt.

As God silently observed Hagar and Ishmael, how grieved He must have been. While He had indeed directed Abraham to exile Hagar and Ishmael, He also loved them. If only they would cry out to Him. If only they would run to Him. If only they would fling their arms of faith around Him. It must have been almost unbearable for God to endure the silence and just watch them suffering, especially when He was right there. But God is patient. He just waited.

I wonder if Hagar's sobs became muffled whimpers as her exhaustion began to take its toll. Did the hot breeze then grow still, the birds stop chirping, and silence grip the desert as if creation itself was holding its breath listening, waiting for even the slightest indication that Hagar or Ishmael would cry out to the God who was there?

Finally, the silence was broken by a raspy sound from a parched throat — but it wasn't coming from Hagar. It came from the direction of the scrub bushes. *Ishmael!* The arrogant, insolent teenager was reaching out to his father's God — the same God who had ...

Renewed His covenant with Ishmael's father, committing
  Himself to Abraham and his family forever,[3]

Accepted Ishmael's claim of a relationship with Him when
  Ishmael had followed Abraham's example and submitted to
  circumcision, the sign of the covenant,[4]

Promised to give Sarah a son of her own,[5]

Listened to Abraham's persistent intercession for Sodom,
  then answered by saving Lot from the judgment that fell on
  the city,[6]

Answered prayer miraculously, delivering Abraham and his
  entire family from a very dangerous situation in Gerar.[7]

I wonder if Ishmael's experience in Gerar came back vividly to his mind. He had been about thirteen years of age at the time. Abraham had taken the family to Gerar after the destruction of Sodom. Afraid of being mistreated by the king, Abraham lied about Sarah, saying she was his sister — a lie that had gotten him into trouble before.[8] The entire family was plunged into a life-threatening situation, which was clearly Abraham's fault. Yet God was standing by. When Abraham prayed, God answered and miraculously delivered them.

Ishmael must have wondered, *Is there any hope at all that the God of my father might hear my cry?* He was in a terrifying situation — lost and dying of thirst in the desert with no idea what to do and where to go next, fast running out of strength and breath and life itself. But if God had heard his father, perhaps God would also hear him. There was only one way to find out. And so Ishmael stopped just crying and started crying out.

The heart of the Father must have leaped with joy! Surely, heaven must have applauded because "God heard the boy crying."[9] What amazing grace!

This aspect of Hagar and Ishmael's story is especially meaningful to me as a parent. Like Abraham's example to Ishmael, the life my parents lived in our home provided some of my most important lessons. I wonder if I am providing those same types of invaluable life lessons to my own children and grandchildren.

When my children — and yours — find themselves in an impossibly hard place — especially as a result of their own wrong choices, wrong words, wrong actions — I wonder what they will remember about the way we handled our own hard places. Have we hidden from them our faults and sin, presenting the façade of a perfect parent? Or have we allowed them to see God's grace in our lives when we don't deserve it — blessing us, answering our prayers, and delivering us from self-inflicted wounds? I wonder if their memories of us in the midst of hard places and difficult situations will hinder them or encourage them to cry out to God.

What I do know from experience is that when I've been involved in a wreck, it has been vitally important not to run away from my Heavenly Father, deny my responsibility, or rationalize my behavior. It's been critical to run to Him, to throw the arms of my faith around Him, and confess my sin. To pour out my heart and tell Him about the trouble I'm in and the mess I've made. Not only have I discovered that He is indeed a prayer-hearing, prayer-answering God, but He has allowed me to be an example for those who are closest to me and whom I love the most ... my own family.

I will never forget my own father's godly example. And Ishmael surely didn't forget Abraham's example, either. Perhaps it was for the very reason that Ishmael cried out that God heard, "and the angel of God called to Hagar from heaven."[10]

But wait a minute. Is that a mistake? Isn't God supposed to answer us directly when we cry out to Him? Why would He call to Hagar when Ishmael was the one crying out? Could it be that Ishmael was crying out to God *for his mother*?

I know God hears the prayers of children for their mothers because I have experienced His answers to my children's prayers for me. One example readily comes to mind. It took place when I was leading my annual seminar at the Billy Graham Training Center at the Cove in Asheville, North Carolina. During the seminar each year, I stay in one of the speakers' cabins and thoroughly enjoy a few mountain hikes as a break from preparing teaching material. In the last few years, I have seen a variety of wildlife, including a mountain lion, a mother bear with three cubs, a wildcat, a bobcat with two kittens, snakes, many deer, and wild turkeys, just to name a few. I have a healthy respect for these creatures and keep my distance, but they don't usually frighten me.

Recently, during my time in the cabin at the Cove, my youngest daughter, Rachel-Ruth, felt burdened for my safety. Although she was over two hundred miles away, she sensed that I was somehow in danger. So she prayed earnestly and passionately for my protection.

Amazingly, she actually named in prayer the very danger she felt I was facing — a threatening black bear.

When we later compared notes, we discovered that I had left my cabin to take a hike at the very time she had been praying. As I closed the cabin door, my eye caught some movement and, when I looked more closely, I saw a large, emaciated, and mangy black bear in the nearby woods. I stood there for a moment, just watching, and then realized the bear was coming straight for the cabin! I ducked back in the door, shut it tightly, and then went to the window. Sure enough, the bear came up onto the cabin porch, knocked over the glass of iced tea I had just left by the rocking chair, and started to maul the pillow I had just been sitting on! When I banged on the window to get him to drop the pillow, he reared up on his hind legs and looked fiercely back at me. As I watched, he circled the cabin three times before he finally meandered off through the woods.

What struck me was that the bear did not seem frightened of me at all. On occasion, I have bumped into bears while hiking, and they have always steered clear of me, and I have done my best to steer clear of them. But this bear looked like he was starving, his behavior was not normal, and I believe he would have come after me had I encountered him on the trail. If I had left the cabin even five minutes earlier, I would have been oblivious to his lurking in the nearby woods and would have been caught outside, exposed to the threat of attack.

This experience brought a double blessing — not only was I saved from danger, but I was also greatly encouraged in the knowledge that my daughter's sensitive and personal prayers on my behalf were heard and answered by God. How remarkable, how astounding, how humbling to think that God hears the cry of our children ... *for us!*

My experience leads me to believe that Ishmael was crying out to God on behalf of his mother. Maybe he even went so far as to confess his faults and acknowledge that he didn't deserve God's mercy. Maybe he pleaded with God on behalf of his mother because he viewed her as the innocent victim of his life-wrecking behavior. Maybe, in the humility born of desperation, his pride, arrogance, and self-centeredness were finally broken as he prayed for someone else. Maybe his cry was voiced in a tone of repentance.

If Ishmael was indeed praying to his father's God, the Bible doesn't give us any details. What it does say is that *God heard the boy crying.*

I *know* God hears the prayers of children for their parents. But I also know that God hears and answers our own prayers, not just those of our children, because He is a prayer-hearing, prayer-answering, miracle-working God.

Wrap your heart and mind around the phrase that's repeated twice in one verse: *God has heard.*[11] God has heard your cries; He has heard the cries of your son or daughter; He has heard the cries of your loved ones and friends and neighbors and any and all who lift up their voices and weep ... to Him.

If you listen carefully, you will hear your Heavenly Father whispering: *I've heard you crying. I've known all along about your wreck ... the tangled, troubled mess in your life. I was watching you when it happened. There is nothing you say or do, no place you go, no person you are with that I don't know about. I was just waiting for you to come tell Me. I love you. I can redeem the wreck and turn the consequences into a blessing if you will surrender them to Me. And in the long run, you will be a better person because of this. Because I am a God who hears and answers prayer. And I can work miracles on your behalf.*

TWELVE

A Stubborn Spirit

*Exile from Him
Is Self-Imposed*

What is the matter, Hagar?

Genesis 21:17

Several years ago I met a handsome, gifted, extremely intelligent young man. William was an investigative journalist for a major newspaper. He came to my attention through an article he'd written describing his journey *away* from God. At the very same time, I had just published *The Magnificent Obsession*, a book about my journey *to* God. In the article, he described himself as a born-again Christian who had felt assured he had a relationship with God. But during the course of his work as a journalist, he had uncovered such hypocrisy in the organized church and among those who called themselves Christians that he had grown increasingly disenchanted. He blamed God for allowing the sin and abuse he had uncovered, and he was unable to separate God from God's fallible people. And so William had walked away from God's people ... and from God. He has since built up something of a speaking and writing career around his professed agnosticism. I bought and read his book that described how he had lost his faith reporting on religion in America and how he had even found unexpected peace in the loss.[1] My heart was grieved, and I began to pray for William each time he came to mind, which was frequently, for over a year.

In looking over my upcoming travel schedule one morning, I noted that I would be in the area where William worked. I asked a staff member to contact him to see if he would be open to having a conversation with me. He agreed. I became increasingly filled with anticipation as it became apparent that God's fingerprints were all over the arrangements. The hotel in which I would be staying was just two blocks from the venue at which he would be speaking on the very same day I had requested a meeting. So . . .

Several weeks later, I found myself looking into William's eyes over a glass of iced tea in the hotel dining room. He was warm, friendly, and not surprisingly, a little guarded. As I tried to put him at ease, I was overwhelmed by an awareness of God's love for William. I could *feel* God's love for him, and I knew William had heaven's undivided attention. I also knew God deeply cared that he had been hurt and wounded by Christians. And so, to the best of my ability, I relayed the message God had put on my heart.

I told William I was so sorry for the way we — God's people — had behaved. I apologized to him for the very real hurt Christians had inflicted on him. I also shared some of the hurts I had experienced. I told him that while we had had similar experiences, we had come to dramatically different conclusions. Rather than drive me away from God, the hypocrisy and sinfulness I had seen in the organized church and in the lives of some of God's people had caused me to run to God, to wrap my arms of faith around His neck, and to cling tightly, knowing He was not like the people who had hurt me. I had made the decision to embrace knowing God as He truly is — not as some people say He might be or think He is or portray Him to be. I recommitted my life to reflecting who God truly is through my own words, actions, and decisions. I did not want to ever be like *them*, the ones who had hurt me. I concluded with an urgent appeal: "William, God loves you. Don't reject Him because others have rejected you or disappointed you. He is not like them. Get to know Him for who He is, not for the tarnished reflection some people give of Him. God desires for you to know Him in a personal, love relationship. Come back to God!"

As we parted, dear William leaned over and kissed my cheek. Although we had a warm rapport and he listened respectfully to what I had to say, I detected no change in his attitude. When I arrived back in my room after our meeting, there were tears on my face — and I believe there were tears on the face of the God who loves him. To my knowledge, William continues to hold to his view that there is no God. While he readily blamed others for the journey that brought him to this final conclusion, I couldn't help but wonder if his prolonged spiritual exile was self-imposed.

I wonder if Hagar also had a stubborn spirit at this stage of her journey that was prolonging not just her physical wandering, but her spiritual exile. It almost seems she would rather die than humble herself and cry out to God ... that she was refusing to see the situation any way but her way. Perhaps she reasoned that if God agreed with Abraham and Sarah, He was in the wrong. Or maybe she concluded, like William, that there really wasn't a God after all. It could be she convinced herself she had been deluded about Him all along.

I've met believers who begin to doubt the presence and power of God in their lives when He doesn't answer their prayers by giving them what they want, in the way they want, when they want. It's as though they demand that He prove Himself to them by coming alongside and carrying out their will, not the reverse. They can't believe a good and loving God would allow them to wander in the wilderness ... to struggle in such a hard and lonely and difficult place. So they conclude that He is not good and loving. Or, if He's not going to do things their way, then they don't want Him. Or they may even conclude that He's not there.

To Hagar, her predicament must have seemed grossly unjust, unrighteous ... *and unbelievable*! Her world was turned upside down and inside out on every level. She was expelled by those who called themselves by God's name, excluded from fellowship with God's people, and now in exile on the brink of destruction. And not for something she had done, but for something her teenager had done. She must have felt stubbornly defiant and justified in remaining silent.

If Hagar suffered from a stubborn spirit, doubted God's power to make a difference, and was therefore deluded about His presence in her life at that moment, her delusion was short-lived. Because in response to Ishmael's cry, God lovingly, patiently, tenderly spoke to her: "What is the matter, Hagar?"[2] I sense a very soft rebuke within the question. God obviously was not questioning Hagar for information. He was seeking to draw a confession from her, prodding her ever so gently to examine her own attitude and actions, saying in effect, *Hagar, why are you so helpless and hopeless? Don't you remember that I am the One Who Sees you? After more than twenty years of living in a relationship with Me, how is it you have forgotten that I am just a prayer away? Why, Hagar, are you not praying? You may be separated from Abraham's household, but you are not separated from Me. I have not left you, even for a moment. I am right here. Your exile from Me, Hagar, is self-imposed.*

Dear believer-in-exile, are God's words to Hagar also God's words to *you*? Is your exile from Him self-imposed? Before you reject that suggestion, it may be worthwhile to think it through for a moment. Since God used a question to get Hagar's attention, ask God to use the following questions to guide your thoughts as you reflect on His presence in your situation. As you do, open the ears of your heart to listen to what He might be saying ...

Do you think God has forsaken you when He says He never will?[3]

Do you think God no longer loves you when He says He always will?[4]

Do you think God no longer cares about you even though He says He most certainly does?[5]

Do you think the wretched way others have treated you is an accurate reflection of how God treats you when He says it is not?[6]

Do you think your situation is beyond His ability to alter when He says He's the God of the impossible?[7]

I wonder how long you have kept God waiting for you to turn to Him in your spiritual wilderness. Surely He weeps as He watches you and me allowing our anger at others to spill over into our relationship with Him, blaming Him for what happened to us, insisting stubbornly that it's His fault, becoming so offended by the people who hurt us that we are also offended by God. Are you hunkered down in your spirit — eyes tightly shut, ears deafened, face turned away from Him — *intentionally*?

Self-imposed exile can become a prison cell that locks from the inside. The key that unlocks the door is a simple one, but potentially a key that is so heavy and painful to lift and use that we look for any other key but that one. But there isn't another one that unlocks the door. The key that works is to cry out to God in humility and sincerity, out of desperate necessity, acknowledging if He doesn't find and save us, we will remain caged in our misery. But to pick up the key we have to lay down our hardness of heart and stubbornness of spirit.

We have to deny our pride. We have to want to come out of exile into the glory of His presence more than we want to remain where we are.

Would you pick up the key? Right now? Throw away your pride. Cry out to God, *Help me! Please!* Come to Him. *Run to Him.* Fling your arms of faith around the neck of your Savior. Ask Him to save you from such a miserable existence. Ask Him to forgive you of your wrongdoing as you stop complaining about theirs. Then ask Him to refill and revive and redirect you according to His plan and purpose for your life.

If you say *no* . . . then your stubbornness must be applauded in hell. Your silence must be deafening in heaven. And surely, as God opens His mouth to speak to you, there must be tears on His face.

If you say *yes* . . . then God will move heaven and earth to come to you. Your exile will be over.

THIRTEEN

The Turning Point

That Was Then,
This Is Now

Do not be afraid; God has heard the boy crying as he lies there. Lift the boy up and take him by the hand, for I will make him into a great nation.

Genesis 21:17 - 18

Diets are difficult for me because I love to eat! I love the taste of food, and I love the comfort food brings. So if I am going to give up food or cut back on food, I have to be hugely motivated. And usually that motivation comes when I either step on the scale or look in the mirror. The moment of truth — that I am carrying more weight than feels or looks good — presents me with a choice. I can continue in my misery and discomfort, hiding my weight under long, floppy clothes and talking about how I need to shed a few pounds, or I can change my eating habits. I have to reach a turning point. I have to want to lose weight more than I want to eat those fried onions, or fried chicken, or fried potatoes, or fried shrimp, or fried okra, or fried green tomatoes, or fried anything. The battle of the bulge is a battle of my will. I have to decide not only that the time has come for a change, but then I have to exercise my will and make the change. Just do it!

The same is true when I experience a wound in my spiritual journey. I have to come to a turning point where I want to be healed more than I want to be wounded. Because, to be truthful, there are some wounds I have nursed. Sometimes it feels good to hurt bad. I can take a wicked pleasure in rehashing what others have said or done to inflict the wound, each time reaffirming my own innocence and giving in to self-pity. I derive a counterfeit comfort from extending to myself sympathy and consolation and understanding. After all, I *deserve* those tears! Yet, even though it is often appropriate to grieve, an attitude of entitlement about my wounds can keep me wandering in a spiritual wilderness, weeping under the scrub bush, getting nowhere with my life. At some point, I have to decide if the wounds are worth holding on to. The wounding is past. That was then; this is now.

I believe Hagar had reached that turning point in her own journey. She had to decide if she was truly ready and willing to change. She had to stop her sobbing, stop fighting the wounders — mentally, emotionally, and spiritually — and just be still. She had to acknowledge the reality of her current position so she could get on with the rest of her life. Regardless of how she arrived where she was, she was there. I wonder if, in her weariness, she was just too tired to even take another step, think another thought, make any decisions at all.

God understands. Years later, another wounded child of His was running for his life through the desert.[1] The prophet Elijah had just miraculously defeated the prophets of Baal on Mount Carmel. He then prayed, and the three-year drought that had plagued his nation ended with a pouring rain. But instead of being grateful for Elijah's powerful ministry, the wicked queen was enraged and put out a warrant for his capture, dead or alive. And so Elijah ran.

When he finally collapsed under a broom tree, Elijah prayed that he might die. He was so exhausted and depleted that he fell asleep. He awoke to a gentle touch from the Angel of the Lord, who had brought him a jar of water and had fresh bread baking over a hot fire. Elijah ate, drank, then went back to sleep. For a second time, the Angel of the Lord touched him. With tenderness and compassion, He conveyed the sympathetic heart of the Father: "Get up and eat, for the journey is too much for you."[2]

If God was sympathetic and compassionate with Elijah, and He was, why do you think He would blame you for your weakness and weariness and woundedness? God understands. But He won't leave you in that depleted place. Elijah was so terrified for his life that, after sleeping and eating, he ran for another forty days. But he couldn't outrun God, who met him at the end of his journey and gently asked, "What are you doing here, Elijah?"[3] In the remarkable encounter that followed, God brought Elijah to a turning point — he had to choose between living in terror or trusting God with his future. Elijah chose to leave behind his fears and sense of failure and move forward to complete the ministry God had for him.

Sometimes we need an extra push to get out of the miry pit in which we've been living. And that's often when God shows up. He seems to wait, quietly and patiently, until He knows we've reached the turning point. Then He gives us that extra incentive, just as He did for Elijah — and Hagar.

God leaned out of heaven and spoke to Hagar. And the first good, healthy choice Hagar made was to listen to the voice of God. Just the sound of His voice revealed that she and Ishmael were not alone after all! She had felt panicked that they would die alone in the desert and she had been convinced there was no one nearby to help. But she couldn't have been more mistaken. God was with her. In spite of her stubborn refusal to cry out to Him, He was calling out to her — by name. *Hagar* ...

His voice must have been like a cool, refreshing breeze blowing from the oasis of His presence, soothing the fear that had gripped her. And His word spoke peace to her heart when He said, "Do not be afraid."[4] Instantly, the turmoil in her heart was replaced by a deep, quiet calm. If Hagar was like me ...

I have experienced the difference God's Word makes when I've been caught in a whirlpool of grief and despair. I will never forget when my son's first marriage ended in divorce after seven years. He was deeply wounded. As in any broken relationship, he was also a wounder. When I first became aware that his marriage was headed for destruction, his pain sent me into a wilderness of guilt. Every parenting mistake I had ever made came back to my mind like the replay of a horror movie in high-definition color. Like Hagar, I curled up into an emotional ball on the inside, blaming myself for all the things I had done wrong — as well as all the things I hadn't done, should've done, could've done to prevent such a living death. Although I cried out to God, my self-flagellation drowned out anything He may have tried to say to me.

Finally, after an all-nighter of emotional turmoil, I was exhausted. As my spirit grew quiet, I slipped out of bed and opened my Bible. These verses fell off the page and into my heart:

> O afflicted one, storm-tossed and not comforted,
> behold I will set your stones in antimony
> and your foundations I will lay in sapphires ...
> your battlements of rubies ...
> your gates of crystal ...
> your entire wall of precious stones.
> [And] your ... son will be taught of the LORD;
> and the well-being of your son will be great.[5]

Like Hagar, I was suddenly aware that God had been right there beside me all night. He knew I had been "storm-tossed" — tossed about by regrets, if-onlys, anger, frustration, grief, and fear. He had heard me sob into my pillow, begging Him to do something. The emotional pain had been so great I didn't think I could catch the next breath.

When He addressed me as the afflicted one who could not be

comforted, He reaffirmed that He knew me intimately, because I had revealed my agony to no one else. I knew His promises — of sapphire foundations, ruby battlements, crystal gates, and walls built with precious stones — spoke of Jerusalem, the home of God's children. But I applied them to my home — that God would make it beautiful, a sparkling jewel-like display of His glory. Then deep peace flooded my heart when God reassured me that my son would be taught of the Lord through the experience of divorce, and in the long run, my son would not only survive, but grow into a stronger, more spiritually healthy person.

I have driven a stake down into that promise and clung to it in the midst of other hurricane-strength storms that have continued to plague our family. As Hagar also discovered, the Word of the Lord has given me peace, even concerning past failures.

If you too are storm-tossed and not comforted, take a deep breath. Could it be that you have not been listening to God's voice? Really listening, with your eyes on the pages of your Bible. I have no doubt that He is right there beside you. Maybe one reason He has allowed you to get sucked into this downward spiral of fearful desperation is to bring you to a turning point. Some people might describe it as the end of the rope. It's that moment when you are so sick and tired of your misery, you are willing to change. If that's where you are, I have good news: you are ready for the next step.

With peace in her heart and God's reassuring words in her ears, Hagar was directed to "lift the boy up and take him by the hand."[6] It was time for her to stop worrying and to start reaching out to her son. She needed to get her eyes off of herself, off of her circumstances, off of her past, and focus on the needs of another. She had to learn that it wasn't all about her — or *them*.

The most poignant example of this antidote to emotional pain was given to us by Jesus Himself as He hung on the cross. He not only suffered physically as He hung nailed to the wooden crossbeams, but He suffered emotionally. Before He was crucified, He was stripped of His clothes. He was crucified, not in a remote, secluded location where He could suffer privately, but publicly beside the main road going into Jerusalem. Instead of a quick, painless death, He endured a slow, torturous, excruciating day of untold agony, nailed to a wooden cross.

So, get the picture: Jesus — Lord of Glory, Bright and Morning Star, Son of God and Son of Man, Lion of Judah, the Creator of Life, the Light of the World, the Messiah — was hung naked from a cross at eye level beside the main road going into Jerusalem, with people walking by on their way to market as they were preparing for Passover. The ones who noticed Him mocked Him for the sign that hung over His head declaring Him King of the Jews. And how did Jesus handle such public humiliation and shame? He turned His attention to others: to His mother, who was lingering near the foot of the cross,[7] and to the repentant thief, who was dying on the cross next to His.[8]

Jesus' example teaches a powerful lesson. He demonstrates that one way to overcome emotional pain is to focus on the needs of others — to reach out and help someone else who may also be suffering. In some way we may not fully understand, helping to alleviate the suffering and pain of someone else actually helps to relieve our own.

The beautiful, tender, and specific instructions God gave to Hagar reveal the deep compassion of His father's heart. Instead of telling Hagar to go get Ishmael some water, or to tell him to stop his bellyaching, or to tell him to get up because it was time to start traveling again, God told Hagar to "lift the boy up and take him by the hand." God knew Ishmael needed the comfort of his mother's physical touch. Sometimes enough has been said, and we just need to reach out and touch that other person. A hug, a hand on the shoulder, or a pat on the back often says more than words. The Lord understood that sometimes even a miracle isn't enough; people need to be touched. And so ...

He not only commanded that the leper be cleansed, He reached out and touched the untouchable.[9]

He healed Peter's mother-in-law of fever when she lay in bed by touching her hand.[10]

He gave sight to two blind men, not only by telling them that their faith had made them whole, but by touching their eyes.[11]

He had compassion on His terrified disciples by coming to them and touching them when they had just seen Him transfigured in glory and had just heard His Father's voice.[12]

Who needs your personal touch? Who is your Ishmael ... someone who needs your helping hand to lift him or her up off the ground? We seem to be so quick to throw money at whomever it is, or call an agency to do something, or ask our church to get involved, or ignore the person completely. But maybe God has placed this person in your life because He knows that you yourself need the lift that comes from lifting someone else. Maybe the act of helping someone else will be the turning point for you.

FOURTEEN

I Can See!

*Your Valley May Be
the Place of Vision*

Then God opened her eyes and she saw a well of water. So she went and filled the skin with water and gave the boy a drink.

Genesis 21:19

I well remember when I found myself in the valley. It was a valley of deep depression, utter exhaustion, and spiritual dryness. Within a period of eight months, all three of my children got married. One month before my son was married, he was diagnosed with life-threatening cancer and had major surgery. Two months later, he began radiation treatment. During that same time period, my mother was rushed to the hospital five times with life-threatening conditions. Each time, I made the four-hour drive to be with her, saw her through the crisis, then returned home. A major hurricane ripped through our city, wrapping our home in 102 downed trees. We were without power for six weeks, and it took us over a year to dig out of the mess. Somehow, in the midst of everything, I maintained my writing and speaking schedule.

Finally, I cried out in desperation. My prayer was something like this: *God, I don't want to quit what I'm doing in ministry. I don't want to escape through taking the pills the doctor offered me or drinking the alcohol people say will relax me. I don't want to go on a vacation where I may be physically rested but return to the same overwhelming circumstances. I'm not even asking You for a miracle. Please, dear God, I need a fresh touch from heaven. I want a fresh encounter with You. Just give me Jesus!*

I can't remember how I was led at that moment. All I know is that I opened my Bible to the gospel of John. I started studying the encounters Jesus had with individuals. As I worked my way through the stories, something happened deep within, and I knew I was encountering Jesus in a fresh way. There was nothing mystical or spooky about it. I was just meeting Him very personally in the pages of my Bible.

And that's when my valley became the place of my vision. Because I looked up in my spirit, and I thought, *If Anne Graham Lotz, a preacher's daughter, could have a desperate heart's cry for a fresh touch from heaven, then could there be other people who have that same heart's cry? People sitting in church, going through the motions of Christian service, outwardly expressing their faith, yet inwardly desperate for something, just not knowing what they were desperate for or how to go about finding it?*

The vision came into focus when God put it on my heart to offer arena-sized events for women called *Just Give Me Jesus*, for the sole purpose of bringing others like myself into a fresh encounter with Jesus through His Word.

So after three false starts over a two-year period, with lots of heartache and struggle and tears, I have now held over thirty-five revivals for the past thirteen years in major cities throughout the United States and the world. Some arenas have overflowed, some have been filled to capacity, some have been half-filled, but in every single arena, *without exception*, God has shown up! People have experienced life-changing revival as they have had a fresh encounter with the invisible Jesus, the Angel of the Lord, the same One who pursued and found Hagar by the spring in the desert.

I doubt that I would ever have had the vision to offer *Just Give Me Jesus* if I had not been in the valley myself.

If you are in the valley, open your eyes to what God may be trying to show you. Don't let your woundedness or weariness blind you to the opportunity God has placed in your path. Let Him open your eyes.

God allowed Hagar to descend to the depths — to be stripped of comfort, security, honor, reputation — until she was literally lying in the dust with nowhere to turn and no one to turn to. She was hemmed in by mountains of sin — Pharaoh's, Abraham's, Sarah's, her own, and Ishmael's. Yet the valley became her place of vision when "God opened her eyes and she saw a well of water."[1]

Did she slowly sit up, smear the dust in streaks across her face as she wiped away her tears, rub her eyes, then look again? Maybe like many desert wanderers before and since, she thought the water that she now saw was a desert mirage playing a cruel trick on her eyes. Maybe she stumbled over to it, certain it would vanish in the desert heat, only to find that she actually could submerge her hand in the coolness and splash her face with the wetness — water! *Water in the desert!* How could that be? How was it she hadn't seen it before? Had the well been there all along but she had been unable to see it because she was blinded by tears? Or had God supernaturally placed it there, bringing water out of the dusty ground as He would later bring water from a desert rock?[2]

While we are not given the answer, we do know that God opened her eyes, enabling her to see something she had not seen previously. And she had to be willing to look — to see an opportunity, a possibility she had not seen before. Then she had to take it.

What is your valley? Is it a valley of . . .

despair or depression or desertion,
humiliation or hopelessness or heartache,
sin or shame or suffering,
loneliness or loss or lovelessness,

frustration or fear or failure,

grief or guilt or _____? You fill in the blank.

Instead of struggling, resisting, beating your fists against the confinement, pain, and injustice, would you look up? Open your eyes. Maybe, just maybe, your valley could become the place of your vision.

When Danny and I left our church in support of the young pastor who we felt had been unnecessarily wounded and mistreated by the elders, we went into exile, as I previously shared with you. Yet had Danny and I not been in that spiritual valley, we would not have had the vision to help plant another church. And without our help, it would have taken the new pastor a lot longer to launch what has become a thriving ministry. And a lot of people whose lives have been radically saved and transformed during those first few years, at the very least, would have postponed their connection to Jesus, which the church helped them to make.

Over and over again in my life, God has brought blessing from brokenness. But first I have to open my eyes to see. In some ways, the wounds themselves can be called a blessing because I've discovered that I need to be wounded in order to offer true comfort to others who have been wounded too.[3] Wounds hurt, but they also ...

deepen my compassion,

strengthen my faith,

refocus my perspective,

enlarge my heart,

broaden my understanding,

and increase my discernment.

Even when I haven't experienced precisely the same wounds that others have, the brokenness and pain in my life seem to soften me and release the sweetness of God's love and grace to others who are suffering.

While writing this very section of Hagar's story, I asked God to open my eyes to others who may be hurting — people to whom I could extend a hand and help to lift up in their spirits. He clearly brought three people to my mind. The first was a woman who has been my Spanish interpreter for over twenty years, who had just finished three months of daily radiation for cancer of the cranium. The second was a young pastor who had recently left a ministry position with the Bowery Mission in lower Manhattan to plant a church in Hunt's Point, the Bronx. The third was a man who had lost his only son in a tragic skateboarding accident nine months previously.

Because each person lived in faraway states, I extended my hand through phone calls. I was able to reach each one the first time I called. I listened to their pain, shared a word of Scripture, shed tears, and prayed with them. At the conclusion of each conversation, I felt the person's spirits were lifted. I do know that I carried all three in my heart throughout the night in prayer. And I am convinced that had I not also experienced the valley firsthand — if I had not been in the pit from time to time in my life — I would not have been able to direct their eyes to the glory of the stars overhead.

I understand what it's like to be so weary and wounded that entering into one more person's suffering is almost more than I can take on. And yet, that very opportunity may bring me relief from my own pain and joy in the midst of my own brokenness. So I pray, *Lord God of Hagar, open my eyes when I'm in the valley.* And He has. And He does.

One morning when I went to buy a cup of coffee, God opened my eyes to see a weary, wounded expression in the eyes of the barista who often served me. When I inquired, her lips trembled, and she rang up my order without responding. Then she called out my order to another woman behind the counter while she motioned for me to step around to the side. She confided that her husband of more than twenty years had just informed her that he was in love with someone else. Adding insult to injury was the fact that he had just signed a new lease with her for their home, even though he knew he no longer loved her or wanted to remain with her. She was trapped. When she investigated canceling the lease and moving so she would not have to live with a man who now openly voiced his passion for another woman, she found it was out of her financial reach. With tears beginning to spill down her cheeks, she said, "Anne, I don't know what to do."

I put my arms around her and we wept together. Then, right in the middle of the coffee house, I called on the God of Hagar to see this dear woman, to hear her cry, and to provide the means to enable her to take care of herself and her teenage son.

Day by day, week by week, I touched base with her when I went into the coffee shop. Once in a while, if there were no other customers in the shop, I asked her how she was doing. Each time, I continued to see the pain in her eyes and the lifeless expression on her face. Again and again, I told her I was praying. I reminded her that sometimes we have to give God time and make room for Him to work.

About six weeks after our initial conversation, I was waiting at the counter for my coffee when she walked out of the back room, came around the counter, and threw her arms around me. With sparkling eyes and radiant face, she told me God had heard her cry and answered her prayers! A local pastor who also frequented the shop had heard of her predicament, presented her need to his church, and the church had made it possible for her to move into a new home with her son. I hugged her again, gave her a high-five, and left rejoicing in the goodness and generosity of God's people who had been Jesus to her, lifting her out of her desert experience and opening her eyes to the joyous comfort of His loving provision.

Several months later, the barista once again greeted me with another broad smile. She shared that she was moving forward with her life in a new, promising career. And she did.

As Hagar "went and filled the skin with water and gave the boy a drink,"[4] she was making the decision not only to open her eyes, but to move forward into the future God had for her. He had not only brought Hagar to a critical turning point, He had given her vision in her valley. But it wasn't just the vision of a well; it was a vision of her future.

As God instructed Hagar to lift Ishmael up, to reach out and touch him, to take him by the hand, He added the startling revelation, "I will make him into a great nation."[5] It almost seemed a quietly spoken postscript given that what she needed most in that moment was water. But that was when her eyes were opened to the promise of hope for their future.

I first read about this kind of hope that is seen from the valley in a little volume that has become a classic, *The Valley of Vision*. The book is a compilation of prayers prayed long ago and written down by Puritan church leaders. I keep it with my Bible in the place where I meet the Lord each morning. These prayers have been a source of rich blessing as they often eloquently express my own feelings and thoughts.[6] The following prayer is one that has helped me understand that sometimes the wounded, broken heart is the blessed, healed heart.

Lord, high and holy, meek and lowly,
Thou hast brought me to the valley of vision,
Where I live in the depths but see Thee in the heights;
Hemmed in by mountains of sin I behold Thy glory.

Let me learn by paradox
    That the way down is the way up,
    That to be low is to be high,
    That the broken heart is the healed heart,
    That the contrite spirit is the rejoicing spirit,
    That the repenting soul is the victorious soul,
    That to have nothing is to possess all,
    That to bear the cross is to wear the crown,
    That to give is to receive,
    That the valley is the place of vision.

Lord, in the daytime stars can be seen from deepest wells,
    And the deeper the wells the brighter Thy stars shine;
Let me find Thy light in my darkness,
    Thy life in my death,
    Thy joy in my sorrow,
    Thy grace in my sin,
    Thy riches in my poverty,
    Thy glory in my valley.[7]

Don't miss the vision in your valley. Ask God to give you eyes to see the stars that shine brightest when you are in the deepest well.

FIFTEEN

Don't Look Back

*You Can't Drive Forward by Looking
in the Rearview Mirror*

God was with the boy as he grew up. He lived in the desert and became an archer. While he was living in the Desert of Paran, his mother got a wife for him from Egypt.

Genesis 21:20-21

D o you find yourself mired in guilt, constantly tormented by the if-onlys of what could have been, should have been, so that your vision of the future is blurred by your unrealized expectations from the past? We can be so bound by bitterness, anger, and resentment that we ruin our lives at present and destroy any hope we might have as we give in to despair. We can even pinpoint by name those who set all of this in motion — the wounders — as we seem to wallow in our unforgiveness.

I recently watched a televised interview with John Ramsey, father of JonBenét Ramsey, the six-year-old who was tragically and mysteriously killed in her own home on Christmas Day in 1996.[1] Her murder remains unsolved to this day. Mr. Ramsey could have justifiably answered yes to the above question. He described the litany of pain he and his family had endured. A few years before JonBenét's murder, his oldest daughter had been killed in a tragic car accident. Added to the excruciating agony of parents losing two beloved daughters were the wounds perpetrated by police and the public at large who blamed him and his wife, Patsy, for JonBenét's death. Twelve years after the murder, DNA evidence absolved anyone in his family of guilt, and the local authorities issued an apology for their inept handling of the case. Tragically, Patsy died of ovarian cancer in 2006, two years before her family was publicly cleared.

After describing so much that he and his family had been through, Mr. Ramsey then made a stunning statement. He said he had forgiven his wounders. And the reason he gave was that forgiveness was a gift to himself. While acknowledging that his forgiveness may have had no impact on those who had wounded him, he said forgiveness set him free to move into the future. And he desired to help others who had been deeply wounded to do the same.

John Ramsey knew what many wounded people seem to miss, and it's this: the danger of looking back is that you cannot see to go forward when you do. If you insist on driving forward by looking in the rearview mirror, you're going to destroy your future and possibly that of your family and loved ones.

This life lesson is illustrated in Abraham's own life when he left his country, family, and friends to move forward into the future God had for him. He took along his nephew, Lot, who had the same opportunity to move into the future that Abraham did. But Lot never really pursued God. He just seemed to be tagging along with Abraham, pursuing adventure. The biblical account of his life gives the impression that he wanted God's blessings — especially the material and financial ones — but he didn't really care as much about a relationship with God.

Lot's priorities led him to immerse himself in the lifestyle of Sodom, a culture so evil and wicked it provoked God's judgment. When God revealed to Abraham the impending destruction of Sodom, Abraham prayed earnestly for the salvation of those who lived there. Although the city of Sodom was beyond redemption, God answered Abraham's prayer by sending His angels literally to drag Lot, his daughters, and his wife out of the city before it was destroyed. The angels gave very clear instructions to Lot and his family: "Don't look back ... or you will be swept away!"[2]

As the earth trembled beneath their feet, the heavens above were opened with the roar of God's wrath, and the fire of His judgment rained down. Everything in Sodom and the neighboring city of Gomorrah was destroyed, including people, buildings, and vegetation. With thick black smoke burning their eyes and sulfur choking their throats, Lot and his family ran for their lives. "But Lot's wife looked back."[3] She just couldn't let go of the life she had been living. And so she lost everything — including her life and God's blessing on her children and grandchildren for generations to come. Lot's wife teaches us that we can't move forward while looking back. If we do, at the very least, we'll stumble.

Hagar now had the opportunity to move forward. She must have staggered to her feet and limped unsteadily over to the well to fill the empty "skin with water and [give] the boy a drink."[4] Surely she splashed water on her face as she drank deeply. As the cooling refreshment began to revive her, I wonder if she had a moment to reflect on what she had just heard. Did God's words begin to sink into her sun-scorched mind? With her brow furrowed and her eyes staring off into the future with concentrated thought, she must have stopped splashing and drinking and begun to ponder what God's words about Ishmael might actually mean.

Years before, when Hagar fled from her abusive mistress, God had promised her that if she would obey Him by returning and submitting to Sarah, He would give her descendants too numerous to count. But what was it that God had just said? In her eagerness to give Ishmael water and to drink some herself, she may not have paid close attention to the promise that was included with the instructions. Did it now come back to her with startling clarity? God had just stated that He would make Ishmael into a great nation.[5] A great nation! That was more than just lots of children and grandchildren. A great nation meant honor, position, respect, and power. That implied they might both have a future with purpose and hope and blessing!

As she surely thought over and over about what God had said, the meaning must have unfolded as quickly in her mind as the bloom on a desert cactus after a spring rain.

Suddenly her hopelessness vanished! And *she knew* ...

That she and Ishmael would not only survive the desert,
> but that they would have a grand and glorious future.

That although God's plan and purpose for Ishmael's life was
> different from that of Isaac's life, it was not a second-rate plan.

That she had not left God back at Abraham's tent, nor had
> He left her.

That God was there for her, and He would always be there — for
> her, for her son, for her grandchildren, and for all of her
> descendants in every generation yet to come.

Hagar's faith, and the hope that came with it for herself and for Ishmael, was now established on God's Word.

Leaving Abraham's household was not the end of everything; it was the beginning of God's unique plan and distinct purpose for Ishmael. Ishmael's life would count for something — he had not missed out on God's blessing for his life after all. The God of Abraham was also the God of Hagar. The God of Isaac was also the God of Ishmael. God was not only the God of the inner circle, but the God of those on the periphery!

Best of all, Hagar now knew with certainty that God loved not only Abraham and Isaac, but also loved her and Ishmael. Hagar's heart surely filled with joy and hope, even as she took Ishmael's blistered, sunburned hand in her own and they walked together into the future. I wonder if she whispered through dry, cracked lips, *Ishmael, listen to me. My God — our God — has seen us, heard us, and provided us with a well of water. And He has given us a promise, Ishmael. Come, we have a future after all.*

There is no evidence that Hagar ever looked back. She did not live bitterly imagining what her life would have been like if she had not been exiled from Abraham's household. She gives every indication that she fully embraced the future God had for her and for her son, even though it was vastly different than what she had imagined it would be. Hagar had to let go of the past and of any plans she may have had for her life in order to enjoy all that God had for her. And so to claim God's promise of descendants and hope for Ishmael's future, Hagar "got a wife for him."[6]

God kept His promise to Hagar. Ishmael married and had a family of his own. Included among his descendants are the majority of the Arab peoples living around the globe today and all Muslims. While many of Ishmael's descendants in our world today live in poverty, no one can dispute that the nations they have established have been richly blessed with almost unlimited natural resources at their disposal. And while many of Hagar's descendants today are suffering, her God is still standing by, patiently waiting ... because God loves them.

But to receive the fullness of God's promise and purpose for herself and her son, Hagar had to proceed through life by looking ahead. She could not go forward by staying focused on the past any more than you and I can drive our cars forward by looking in the rearview mirror.

When you and I were young, we often had a picture of what we wanted our lives to be like when we grew up ... a picture of our career, our family, and our children. What did you imagine your life would be like today? Has the canvas of your life's painting turned out as you expected? Or has it been marred — slashed by a handicap, hurts, injustice, illness, bankruptcy, betrayal?

The way to healing, the way to freedom from the wretchedness of the pain, is *not* revenge. It is not giving *them* — the ones who wounded you — the silent treatment, or cutting them off, or cutting them out. It is not rejecting God and losing your faith. It is not blaming others and claiming to be an innocent victim. Vengeance, slander, self-defense, finger-pointing, and blame-giving will not ease your pain. God tells us exactly how to be healed. The remedy is simple but radical: "Bear with each other and forgive whatever grievances you may have against one another. Forgive as the Lord forgave you."[7]

Would you be willing to forgive? To release your hurt to God by forgiving those who have hurt you? Often that's the last thing you and I would ever think of doing. Somehow we're afraid that if we forgive them, they will somehow get away with what they have done to us. By holding on to our anger, we feel we are somehow making God pay for what He has allowed. But those very injustices and wounds God allows into our lives can go beyond hurt and become spiritually self-destructive if we refuse His healing remedy. Remember, you can't move forward while looking backward.

I was reminded in a fresh way of the need to forgive in order to move forward at the end of a recent dinner conversation with two couples, both of whom had held strategic leadership positions within Christian organizations and had been deeply wounded. One couple had pastored a large, influential church, only to be moved out because they had become "too evangelical." The husband of the other couple had held the presidency of a Christian college but had been removed when he was caught up in a power struggle within the board of directors. We had finished our meal when one of the women mused rather wistfully, "Anne, one day when we have time, I would like to ask you about forgiveness." Then she paused for a moment, took a deep breath as though drawing in courage, and said, "Actually, I want to ask you now." I was somewhat familiar with the circumstances of the extremely painful and humiliating experience she and her husband had endured at the hands of Christian leaders on the board of directors, so I shot up a silent arrow prayer, asking God to give me His insight and wisdom. I knew she was trying to move forward but was struggling to overcome this major obstacle. She was asking for help.

She related that someone had told her she had to forgive those who had essentially erased twenty-seven years of accomplishment from her husband's life. Of course, she affirmed, she knew she was supposed to forgive.[8] But then the person who told her she needed to forgive added something else — that the evidence of her forgiveness would be when she could love the wounders as God loved them. The look in her eyes tightened slightly as she confessed, "I don't think I can do that." While I knew she and her husband had moved forward professionally by taking another prominent leadership position, I knew also she was personally and spiritually stuck in the quicksand of wounds from her past.

I candidly responded that if I were in her shoes, I couldn't love the wounders as God loved them either — not in myself. C. S. Lewis wrote, "Love is not an affectionate feeling, but a steady wish for the other person's ultimate good as far as it can be obtained."[9]

Love is a choice — a decision we make to put the well-being of the other person before our own. And forgiveness is also a decision. It is not pretending that I have not been wounded or saying that what the other person did was not wrong. It is not letting them get by with it by not holding them accountable.

I have been asked repeatedly, "Anne, how have you experienced healing of your wounds? How have you been able to move past them?" The answer, which may seem simplistic but is the one that works, is that the healing antidote to wounds is forgiveness. But I don't stop with just the decision to forgive. Once I have made the decision to forgive, I move forward by doing something for the person who has hurt me.

I've learned that forgiveness is an intellectual choice I am commanded to make. If it were a feeling or an emotion, I couldn't obey the command since I can't necessarily control my emotions and feelings. It's a choice, pure and simple. If I only offered forgiveness to those who ask for it, or those who deserve it, or those I feel like forgiving, there are, to be honest, some people I would never forgive. But it's a decision that I make because I am commanded to forgive for one simple reason: God has forgiven me. As an act of grateful worship, I choose to forgive others.[10]

But then my decision to forgive needs to be followed with an act of love that's sacrificial in nature. I need to do something for the person I am forgiving — something that is costly. Something I would do for no other reason than it's my act of worship — worship of One who laid down His life for me as His own act of sacrificial, loving forgiveness.

As dessert was served, I shared with my friend the story I related in chapter 8 about choosing to be rebaptized when my church canceled the Bible class I taught. I had already made the choice to forgive the church for removing Danny and me from leadership and teaching. My submission to immersion baptism was my way of acting out my forgiveness with a demonstration of sacrificial love. Although it seemed to make no difference to the church, I know it made a difference in me because to this day I harbor no ill-will, bitterness, or unforgiveness. I have just let those feelings go. In fact, I recently found myself in a working relationship with the very man who had presided over the congregational meeting when my husband was removed from church leadership. I didn't find it difficult to work with him because, over time, my choice to forgive years ago had led to authentic feelings of forgiveness.

As the couple sat quietly, their coffee getting cold in cups that went unnoticed, I sensed they were truly listening. So I continued. I shared the testimony of a dear friend, Barb,[11] whose mother had never ceased to find fault with her. Ever since Barb was a little girl, her mother had criticized everything she did. Barb told me that months before Christmas every year, she began to feel nauseated because selecting the expected gift was so traumatic. It didn't matter what the gift was, her mother would not be pleased. Barb dreaded Christmas for that reason alone.

Barb and her mother were involved with other family members in a business venture. One particular year, Barb's mother actually took out a lawsuit against her involving the business. At the same time, Barb's mother was moving out of the home she'd had for decades and into a condominium — and Barb was helping her move! As if that weren't enough, Barb was a fabulous seamstress and she sewed the drapes and other things for her mother's new home.

Barb had dropped by my house one morning, and I remember looking incredulously at her. She was standing on my front steps when I challenged her bluntly, "Barb, how can you do it? How in the world can you help your mother, sew for her, do these other things, while she is suing you in court?" I will never forget Barb's response. She taught me a life's lesson that I was able to share with those at the dinner.

"Anne, I've forgiven my mother," she replied. "But I have to tell you, every time my mother comes to mind, every time I see her or hear the sound of her voice, I have to forgive her all over again. Jesus has taught me to forgive seventy times seven — to place no limits on my forgiveness. But when I made the decision to forgive her, I also made the decision to love her sacrificially. Helping her is my way of showing her I've forgiven her and that I love her. And actually, it has helped me let go. I have been set free from bitterness, anger, and resentment."

I looked at Barb's gentle expression, the light of joy in her eyes, and I knew she was speaking the truth. She was free — free to forgive, free to love. Her wounds had been healed!

When dinner had concluded and we were walking to our cars, the husband of the woman who had asked the question slipped up beside me, put his arm around my shoulders, and whispered, "Thank you. Thank you for your ministry to us tonight." From the look on his face, I was led to believe he had taken the first step out of exile. He was ready to move forward.

Don't underestimate the power of forgiveness in your own life. While others may remain distant, hardened, cold, vengeful, and give only a negative response to your forgiveness — if they give any response at all — the very act of forgiveness fleshed out in sacrificial love will begin the healing process *in you*. And sometimes it does make a difference in the other person.

Although there was no evidence at the time, Barb's forgiveness and love softened her mother's heart. As Barb chose to move forward, within a few years, she had the privilege of leading her mother to receive God's love by placing her faith in Jesus Christ for her own forgiveness. Shortly thereafter, her mother stepped into eternity. I can't even imagine how different Barb's outlook would be now if she had not made the decision to forgive and then move forward by loving her mother *for God's sake.*

Here is the biblical foundation for Barb's lesson: "This is how we know what love is: Jesus Christ laid down his life for us. And we ought to lay down our lives for our brothers ... Dear children, let us not love with words or tongues but with actions and in truth ... And this is his command: to believe in the name of his Son, Jesus Christ, and to love one another as he commanded us."[12]

And that love often involves forgiveness and sacrifice, doesn't it? There never has been, is, or ever will be a greater demonstration of sacrificial love than when *Jesus Christ laid down His life for us.* For you. For me. And He made this sacrifice at a time when we could not have cared less because we didn't even know we were sinners, much less that we needed a Savior who would offer us forgiveness through His own shed blood on the cross.

I shared this principle with Jay, another friend who had been deeply wounded.[13] He was a United States senator who was considered such a strong candidate in his reelection bid that he almost ran unopposed. But at the last minute, another person in the other party declared his candidacy. Millions of dollars in out-of-state revenue was raised by a senate colleague for Jay's challenger. A national marketing team was engaged for the opposition that played loose with the truth, twisting and distorting Jay's record. Jay lost the race.

When I had the opportunity to talk with Jay two years after the disastrous election, I could clearly see the hurt that was still in his eyes. He candidly asked me how he could move past the wound when his political career had been terminated so unfairly. He acknowledged that he struggled with bitterness. So I shared with Jay the principle of making the choice to forgive, then following it with a sacrificial act of love for the wounder.

Several months later, Jay shared that he had gone home and thought through what I had shared. As a result, he had made the decision to forgive his Senate colleague. Then, he had heard his colleague's wife was dying of cancer. So Jay wrote a warm note to tell his former colleague he was praying for them both and sent a gift to express his concern. Jay didn't know if the colleague had been touched, but Jay himself was set free from bitterness. He was no longer looking back, but moving forward, ready to embrace the future that God had for him, which was different than the one he had envisioned for himself.

Although you may not be in exile physically — you may still be going to church, attending Bible studies, involved in religious activities — could it be that your spirit is nonetheless in exile because you are stuck in the quicksand of past wounds? Is there a cold vacancy where there used to be a warm vibrancy of love for the things and people of God? Is there a root of bitterness that is strangling your spirit on the inside, threatening to choke off the future God has in store for you?

Our Lord Jesus Christ, Creator of everything, Lord of Glory, Son of God, the Angel of the Lord who had pursued, comforted, and helped Hagar, gives us a dramatic life lesson on forgiveness by His own example. When He was stripped of His clothes, nailed to the cross with spikes driven through His hands and feet, He prayed, "Father, forgive them, for they do not know what they are doing."[14] If He could forgive the very ones who crucified Him, how can you and I withhold our forgiveness from those who wound us? But He didn't just make the choice to forgive them; *He died for them!*

I recently heard a statement attributed to my dear friend Crawford Loritts.[15] It was based on the account of Jesus' appearance to His disciples in the upstairs room following His resurrection. Jesus showed the disciples His wounds and invited them to reach out and touch them.[16] Crawford remarked that perhaps one reason Jesus did this was to show His disciples that, while scars may remain, wounds can be healed. Quickly. You don't necessarily need years of therapy and counseling.

Perhaps what you need more than anything is a fresh encounter with the risen Lord Jesus Christ. Take a good look at the wounds He bore for you. His decision to forgive you was followed by sacrificial love in action. He died *for you!*

If you are struggling in your effort to move forward because you can't seem to get your eyes off the past, look up. Heed the example of the One who made the decision to forgive His wounders, then followed His decision with a supreme act of sacrificial love.

And don't forget to look ahead. While Jesus will always bear in His body the marks of Calvary, He moved on into all that His Father had for Him after the cross. He walked out of the grave into the glory of heaven and the crown that awaited Him as "King of kings and Lord of lords."[17]

So ... "I keep asking that the God of our Lord Jesus Christ, the glorious Father, may give you the Spirit of wisdom and revelation, so that you may know him better. I pray also that the eyes of your heart may be enlightened in order that you may know the hope to which he has called you."[18] Look up! Look ahead! Don't miss the future God has for you because you keep looking back.

SIXTEEN

It's Time to Move On

You Can Be Reconciled

Altogether, Abraham lived a hundred and seventy-five years.
Then Abraham breathed his last and died at a good old age,
an old man and full of years; and he was gathered to his people.
His sons Isaac and Ishmael buried him in the cave of Machpelah
near Mamre, in the field of Ephron son of Zohar the Hittite,
the field Abraham had bought from the Hittites. There Abraham
was buried with his wife Sarah.

Genesis 25:7 – 10

Wounding smashes relationships. We can never return to the way we were before the wounding took place, which in itself adds a dimension to our grief that is very deep. Yet it is possible for severed relationships to be reconciled.

For years, I had a best friend. We talked almost every day by phone and took every opportunity we could to spend time together, blending our families into lots of happy confusion for picnics, holidays, and special times. But one day I found myself helplessly standing by as my friend was deeply wounded by another, then chose to retaliate. She had many friends and family members cheering her on. But in obedience to what God put on my heart and seeking to be faithful to the insight I felt He had given me, I warned her of the consequences of her actions. While she was justified in her course of action, the long-term repercussions, I believed, would be exceedingly destructive, not only to her, but also to her children.

What I said was not what she wanted to hear. And so she severed our relationship and followed through on her decision to wound the wounder. Like fire hitting a fan, the sparks of her retaliation flew in all directions, burning hearts and hopes and homes and families and futures. While in one sense she had every right to do what she did, it turned out to be devastating. All I could do was weep and pray from a distance. The ache in my heart was almost a physical pain.

Years later, she sat at my kitchen table and, in a voice choking with emotion, tearfully said how sorry she was. She asked for my forgiveness, saying she wanted our relationship restored to what it had been. I wept too. I put my arms around her and hugged her, telling her I had forgiven her years earlier.[1] I told her how much I appreciated her courage in coming to try to make things right. To reconcile. But I knew, even as we opened our hearts to each other, that we could never really go back and reclaim the relationship that had been. It was gone. However — and this is the encouragement I want to pass on to you — we remain good friends to this day. The relationship is different but sweet. I believe it has been healed because she was willing to die to her pride, to humble herself, and to ask for my forgiveness.

I recently came across a quote from John Ortberg that makes a helpful distinction between forgiveness and reconciliation: "You might distinguish between forgiveness as letting go of my right to hurt you back and reconciliation as that which requires the sincere intentions of both parties."[2] The amazing conclusion to Hagar's story is that reconciliation seems to have taken place between both parties ... between her son, Ishmael, and Sarah's son, Isaac.

The Bible doesn't tell us if Hagar ever saw Abraham and Sarah again. But we are given a tantalizing glimpse of a possible reconciliation that took place when Abraham "breathed his last and died at a good old age, an old man and full of years; and he was gathered to his people. His sons Isaac and Ishmael buried him."[3] Isaac *and* Ishmael — *together again*?

How I would love to know ... had Isaac and Ishmael stayed in touch throughout the years? Had they met each other's wives? And shared meals with each other's families? Did they ever go hunting together? Were they cordial and friendly? When Abraham died, was it natural for Ishmael to participate in the funeral? Or had Isaac and

Ishmael not seen each other or spoken since that dreadful day so long ago when Abraham exiled Hagar and Ishmael? If so, what would make Isaac reach out to Ishmael after so many years? In sending word to Ishmael about Abraham's death, was he trying to reconcile with his half brother? Or was Isaac just doing what he felt was right and proper in notifying Abraham's firstborn of his death? Maybe Isaac's gesture was perfunctory, a dutiful effort to honor his deceased father whom he knew had deeply loved Ishmael. I wonder, did Isaac ever imagine that Ishmael would actually show up? But Ishmael did!

In asking Ishmael to come to the funeral, Isaac ran the risk of opening an old wound. But sometimes wounds that have not healed properly need to be lanced, or reopened, in order to purge an infection and allow deep healing to begin. As unpleasant as the thought may be, the wounds from your past may need to be revisited to truly heal.

My nine-year-old granddaughter, Sophia, somehow got a splinter in the back of her hand — a year ago! She wouldn't let anyone, from her mother to her father to me to the pediatrician, touch the painful wound. A couple of weeks ago, we all noticed that the splinter was festering and had raised a blister on her hand that was becoming more and more painful. Finally, my daughter had had enough. She told Sophia to hold still and then pulled out the protruding splinter with her fingers. Sophia yelped at the sudden, sharp pain, but then smiled with relief as the pain she had lived with for over a year was almost instantly eased. A couple of days later, there wasn't even any inflammation to indicate that the splinter had ever been under Sophia's skin.

Wounds can be like Sophia's splinter. We think we can live with them, but they don't seem to go away on their own. Even small ones.

Sometimes we have to reopen the wound in order to extract what's causing the pain so that we can truly heal.

Some time ago, I talked with a handsome, gray-haired gentleman named David,[4] who opened up in a surprisingly vulnerable way. He shared with me that he had been raped when he was about twelve years old by a babysitter who was considered by his community to be a mature Christian. For years, David carried that horrific wound as a secret deep within his heart. But the wound eventually began to fester. The guilt and shame surfaced at unexpected times in fits of rage and ultimately led to alcoholism and drug abuse.

When he surrendered his life in a deeper way to Jesus, David felt led, as an adult, to confront his rapist. And so he did. When they met, David described what had happened between them and then extended grace and forgiveness. But the rapist vehemently rejected David's offer, insisting that the rape had never taken place. Grieved, David drove home, got on his knees, and revisited in prayer the hateful scene that had replayed in his memory so many times. Only this time, he imagined Jesus present in his childhood room, looking at him with infinite tenderness and forgiveness and the deep empathy of One who understands what it feels like to be brutalized.[5] And through a truly supernatural, fresh touch from God, the wound that had been excruciatingly painful for years, and even more painful to reopen, was healed.

If the person who has wounded you, or has been wounded by you, rejects your forgiving words or gestures and refuses to move toward reconciliation, take it to Jesus in prayer. He understands what it feels like to make every effort to reconcile, only to be rejected. The relationship may never be reconciled, but Jesus can heal you — and your memories.

Isaac and Ishmael surely had vivid memories of the wounding that led to their separation. If there had been no contact between the brothers since Hagar and Ishmael were exiled — some seventy years — I wonder what the scene was when they finally met face-to-face. Did they stare at each other awkwardly, shifting from one foot to the other? Did they formally shake hands? Did they politely embrace as they kissed first one cheek, then the other in the custom of the Middle East? Did Ishmael say, "I'm sorry"? Or did they just exchange a long, knowing glance that needed no words? Maybe it was enough that Ishmael had come to help bury their father — in the very same cave where Abraham had buried Sarah years earlier. Sometimes reconciliation begins with just a small gesture, doesn't it? A tiny tendril of contact. Someone who is willing to take the first step, make the first move, say the first word.

If you have a relationship that has been shattered by wounds, would you be willing to reach out to the wounder as Isaac did to Ishmael? Just a small gesture. It can be a brief phone call, a birthday card, an anniversary remembered, a small gift, a few words spoken at a social gathering, warm eye contact instead of a cold stare. Take some action to let the person know you are reaching out, that the door is cracked open to reconciliation. You may never know if the relationship can be reconciled unless you make the effort to begin the process.

On the other hand, is there someone who has been trying to reach out to you? Have you been on the receiving end of a small gesture? At this stage in your journey, perhaps it no longer matters who was the wounder and who was the wounded. What matters is the fact that the person is reaching out and you need to respond. Why won't you? Don't make it hard for someone to come to you.

In time, there will need to be more than just a gesture. There may need to be a face-to-face, heart-to-heart, honest conversation in which you listen to the other person's story and he or she listens to yours. Who knows? Maybe you will discover that a significant part of the problem was miscommunication or misinformation. Even if the conversation reveals you were dead wrong or the other person was totally at fault, you need to give voice to your apology or forgiveness. Don't let pride keep you from genuine reconciliation. And that's where death comes in, isn't it? Death to our pride.

I know I have been a wounder. And I have been wounded. What I also know is that if there is any hope of reconciliation in the relationships that have been severed, someone needs to make the first move. My pride would defensively protest, *They need to come to me. What they did to me was far worse than anything I ever thought of doing to them. I didn't mean to wound them, but they intentionally tried to destroy me. They need to set their wrongs right first.* So there has to be a death. Just as Abraham's death seems to have triggered the reconciliation between Isaac and Ishmael, death is the trigger for reconciliation between my wounders and me. *My* death. I have to die to my pride and my position as the one whose forgiveness should be sought by them.

I need to be easily approachable, as Jesus has been for me.

I need to love those who have rejected me, as Jesus loved me.

I need to initiate the contact, as Jesus did for me.

I need to extend forgiveness to them before they even ask me
    for it, as Jesus did for me.

And so I have. I have tapped softly on the door of hope for a new beginning — a brief phone call, an email, a cup of coffee shared at Starbucks, a memory in the form of a gift tucked in the mail. Has every relationship been healed and reconciled? No. Why not? I have asked myself that more times than I can count. While some relationships have eased into friendship, others remain severed. I'm not even sure that some of my wounders have recognized my gestures for what they were. One thing I do know is that some things take time. I can't force reconciliation. I can't change someone else's heart or mind. Only the Lord can do that. And so I continue to pray and wait.

As I wait, I seem to see with the eyes of my heart that same mysterious figure who hovered in the shadows of Hagar's life, the Angel of the Lord. I'm reminded that He understands what it feels like to wait for those who've wounded Him to respond to His overtures for reconciliation. I know He truly feels my pain.

But this time, He's not looking at me. I imagine Him gazing past me with an expression of infinite tenderness and longing. He's looking at you. He not only made the first move toward you when He left His throne in heaven, came to earth, and went to the cross, but He put this book in your hands. Now He's waiting. Waiting for you to respond and walk through the door He has opened with His nail-scarred hand. A door that leads into reconciliation with His Father and with Himself and, in time, with *them* — the ones who wounded you. Like Isaac and Ishmael, it's a reconciliation that has been made possible through death . . . His death. You can be reconciled when you meet Him — and your wounders — at the foot of the cross.

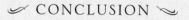

The End of
the Healing Journey

It's Time to Come Home

Come to me, all you who are weary and burdened, and I will give you rest.

The Spirit and the bride say, "Come!" And let him who hears say, "Come!"

So he got up and went to his father. But while he was still a long way off, his father saw him and was filled with compassion for him; he ran to his son, threw his arms around him and kissed him.

Matthew 11:28; Revelation 22:17; Luke 15:20-21

Sunday, June 10, 2012, would have been my mother's ninety-second birthday. While she celebrated in heaven, I wanted to celebrate with my father. Because of a recent trip to India, a subsequent illness, and an overloaded schedule, I had not been to see him for almost two months. So the weekend of Mother's birthday, I drove the four hours home in bumper-to-bumper traffic. The exertion of the drive was more than worth it, not only because I love being with my father anytime, but because of how he welcomed me. When I walked into the house, put my things down, and went back to his quarters, I called out, "Daddy." As I walked into his room, his face lit up, he threw out his arms, gave me a strong, warm embrace, and then kept holding me. He knew that even though I am a grown woman, when I come home I'm just a little girl at heart who loves to be held by her father. In the midst of all of life's stress, struggles, pressures, pain, and problems, there's something for me that's healing in my father's love.

I wonder ... have you been separated from your Heavenly Father for a while? Maybe you've taken a trip to a distant country, a place where you have lived in a way that is contrary to a life that pleases Him.[1] Maybe your wounds have made you sick in bitterness or shame or guilt. Maybe you're apprehensive about seeing Him because you don't think He wants to see you. Maybe you've been so busy with an overloaded schedule that He's been crowded out of your life. Maybe you don't know exactly why, but you just haven't felt your Father's love for a while. For quite a while.

It's time to put your things down — your busyness, fears, doubts, apprehensions, guilt, uncertainties — and enter into His presence on your knees. In prayer. Cry out to Him. Call Him by name, *Abba . . . Daddy*.[2] Experience His arms of love wrapped around you, holding you close, because your Heavenly Father loves you. There is healing in His warm embrace. It's time to come home!

Maybe you are afraid that after years of wandering, burdened with painful memories and all the emotional and spiritual baggage involved, you somehow *can't* come home. That it's too late, that your Father won't receive you, that you have forfeited His blessing in your life, that His love for you somehow over time has been diminished. But dear wounded one, you are the reason He got up from heaven's throne, took off His glory robes, and came into the wilderness of this world. Because He saw you in your hopeless, helpless, wounded condition and came to seek you, to draw you to Himself, and to give you abundant, eternal life. He yearns to hear your voice calling His name so that He can wrap you in His love and fill you with His joy and peace.

Recently, I was with a beautiful young woman who acknowledged her inner agony when she confessed not only to being wounded, but to being a wounder. She had had two abortions that had rendered her unable to conceive a baby she now was desperate to have. But greater than her insatiable longing for a child were her feelings of shame and guilt. She was convinced that her decisions, made years ago out of ignorance and desperation, now prevented her from ever being accepted by God. She was certain that God's punishment for her actions was that she would be childless the rest of her life. The expression on her face was one of utter hopelessness.

While this young woman has yet to have a baby, she does now

have hope. She learned that although there are consequences to our choices, nothing can ever separate us from God's love. And He does not punish us for our sin by withholding a baby or any good thing from us. The wages of sin is death — not our own, but the death of His own dear Son in our place. So she tearfully opened her heart to Him and made the decision to stop looking back and to move forward instead. The same face that had expressed such hopelessness now is softened with the light of His presence. And while she still longs and prays for a baby, she has embraced the magnificent obsession of knowing God and desires His purpose for her life. His love has healed her heart.

God is the God who loves sinners. He loves the wounders and the wounded. He is the God of second chances — and third and fourth! Rather than rejecting you, He seeks you and draws you into His loving arms so that you might be healed of your wounds. God gives hope when there is no hope because God loves you. He truly loves you! You have not been deluded. He is right here. Right there. With you. *Now.* But to experience the fullness of His healing love, you must close the door on your past.

When I was a teenager, I had horses that I kept at a place called Phillips Farm. To get to the barn, I had to drive down a dirt road that led through a corn field. On the far side of the corn field was a gated fence that surrounded a cow pasture. One of the instructions old Mr. Phillips gave me when I boarded my first horse on his farm was that I had to make sure I closed the gate behind me when I left the barn. Otherwise, the cows in back of me could get out of the fenced-in pasture and ruin the corn in front of me.

Dear wounded one, it's time to close the gate behind you. Don't let the memories and the mistreatment, the words and the wounds, the jealousy and the hypocrisy, the deceit and the dishonesty, the cheap talk and the inconsistent walk, the meanness, unkindness, rudeness, pridefulness, selfishness, sinfulness, injustice, and unfairness of people from your past creep into the present and ruin the promise of blessing and hope for the future. Don't let *them* inflict the ultimate wound at the end of your life, when you discover that your life has been wasted. Shriveled. Less than God intended. Because *you* refused to close the gate. So ... close it.

Let go of the past so that you can move forward into all that God has for you.

Let go of your resentment over the way you've been treated.

Let go of your bitterness toward others who have misrepresented God to you.

Let go of your unforgiveness of those who have hurt you.

Let go of your hardened heart toward those who have rejected you.

Let go of the overwhelming desire to justify what you did and explain what they did.

Let go of your vengeful spirit.

Let go of your offense with God because He allowed you to be wounded.

Let go of the life of your dreams that is less now because of them. *Just let go!*

Never mind the injustice and hurt and confusion and fear and loneliness and emptiness and dryness and woundedness. Let go of yesterday.

That was then. This is now.

God is calling you today. I can hear His still, small voice echoing through the story of Hagar, an Egyptian slave, wounded by God's people, a believer in exile, when she wandered in the wilderness: *What's the matter? Do not be afraid. I've heard your heart's cry.* Your cry has reverberated all the way up to heaven and back down into My heart. I've written this book for *you.*

God has a wonderful plan for your life from this day forward, just as He did for Hagar.[3] To possess it, you must do what Hagar did. Let go of the past so you can embrace the future God has for you, especially when it's different from the future you had planned. Come to the end of your healing journey by forgiving those who have wounded you. Those who have marred the picture you had of the life you had wanted to live. Love them, not just in word, but by doing something for them that's sacrificial in nature. Then let go. Enjoy being free at last! Healed at last! Never mind *them*, whoever they are. It's time for *you* to move on. Embrace all that God has for you from this day forward! Embrace the One Who Sees you. The One who's been pursuing you. The One who even now is waiting for you to whisper His name ...

Quarried Deep

The personal stories I have shared with you in this book are the small tip of a larger and ugly iceberg. The wounds in my life run deep in almost every area — family, church, ministry, and community. I have not shared some of the more severe ones out of concern that if I did, I would in turn become a wounder. Again.

I am convinced that were it not for the utter sufficiency of God's grace, mercy, and power to bind up my wounds and heal my broken heart, I would be just a shadow of a person. But instead of lashing out, fighting back, or crumbling, I have embraced the pain. I have asked God to use it to furrow me deep. And He has. I am getting stronger in my faith and growing deeper in my trust of Him for this simple yet profound reason: God is *with* me, His Spirit is *within* me, and His Son is *going before* me.

I can honestly say that I love Him more and trust Him more, *because* I've been wounded. I know that at the end of all things, He will make everything right. He will sort out the motives, the accusations, the betrayals, the jealousies, the deceptions, the slander, the lies, the gossip. This frees me to get on with my life, living each moment for an audience of One.

But I will also admit that from time to time I have cried out to

God, "Lord, did You see that? Did You hear that?" And I know that He has. His answer to me has been simple and repeated over and over again: "Vengeance is Mine. I will repay ... You too be patient; strengthen your heart, for the coming of the Lord is at hand. Do not complain ... against one another, that you yourself may not be judged; behold, the Judge is standing right at the door."[1]

The Judge is at the door. God will settle accounts. But perhaps not just yet. From time to time I remind myself of the two farmers who were gazing out at their fields of wheat that were ready for the October harvest. One farmer was an agnostic who didn't believe in God, never went to church, and worked as hard on Sunday as he did the other six days of the week. The second farmer was a devout Christian who always went to church and never worked on Sunday. The first farmer mocked the second one because he said his field and seven-day work week had yielded more grain, proving that it did not pay to honor God. The second farmer thought for a moment, then drawled, "Well, God don't settle all of His accounts in October!"

God may not settle His accounts on our timetable, but He will settle His accounts. The Judge is at the door. Jesus is coming! So I will be patient as I leave vengeance to Him. I, for one, do not want Him to return and find me licking my wounds, plotting revenge, holding a grudge, or trying in some other way to go forward by looking in the rearview mirror.

I am encouraged by the apostle Paul who said that he bore in his body the marks of the Lord Jesus — that he had been crucified with Christ and had a thorn in the flesh.[2] Those are all wounds. But he didn't get mired in his woundedness, because he was clearly pursuing his goal. While sitting in prison, arrested unjustly for preaching the Gospel, here is how he described his life's ambition: "I want to know

Christ and the power of his resurrection and the fellowship of sharing in his sufferings, becoming like him in his death ... Forgetting what is behind and straining toward what is ahead, I press on toward the goal to win the prize for which God has called me heavenward in Christ Jesus."[3]

Paul's wounds furrowed him deep, and the faith that took root and grew in his life has borne abundant eternal fruit for two thousand years. Without wounds in his life — or in mine or in yours — he and we would remain shallow, living on the surface of our relationship with God, and barren of any eternal, spiritual fruit. One of the early Puritan writers was convinced of this, also, and his beautiful prayer, which follows, expresses my heart's desire to be "quarried deep." And that requires pain. Even as a field is wounded by the plough that turns over the soil in preparation for planting seeds, my life needs to be ploughed deep — wounded, even to the depths of "death."[4] So this is my prayer. Make it yours too ...

> *Lord Jesus,*
> *Give me a deeper repentance,*
> > *A horror of sin,*
> > *A dread of its approach;*
> *Help me chastely to flee it,*
> > *And jealously to resolve that my heart*
> > > *shall be Thine alone.*
> *Give me a deeper trust,*
> > *That I may lose myself to find myself in Thee,*
> > > *The ground of my rest,*
> > > *The spring of my being.*
> *Give me a deeper knowledge of Thyself*
> > *As Saviour, Master, Lord, and King.*

Give me deeper power in private prayer,
*   More sweetness in Thy Word,*
*   More steadfast grip on its truth.*
Give me deeper holiness in speech, thought, action,
*   And let me not seek moral virtue apart from Thee.*
Plough deep in me, great Lord,
*   Heavenly Husbandman,*
*   That my being may be a tilled field,*
*   The roots of grace spreading far and wide,*
*   Until Thou alone are seen in me,*
*   Thy beauty golden like summer harvest,*
*   The fruitfulness as autumn plenty.*
I have no Master but Thee,
*   No law but Thy will,*
*   No delight but Thyself,*
*   No wealth but that Thou givest,*
*   No good but that Thou blessest,*
*   No peace but that Thou bestowest.*
I am nothing but that Thou makest me,
I have nothing but that I receive from Thee,
I can be nothing but that grace adorns me.
Quarry me deep, dear Lord,
*   And then fill me to overflowing*
*   With living water.*[5]

Lifted Up

*In his love and mercy he redeemed them;
he lifted them up and carried them ...*

Isaiah 63:9

This book has not been easy to write. As I have reflected on my life's experiences to find examples to share with you, the Holy Spirit has brought wounds to mind that had long been forgotten. In each case, I had to revisit the scene and forgive the wounders — my fifth-grade teacher, the boarding school staff, and others I've written about. So writing this book has been something of a healing journey for me. But it's a journey that, in all honesty, lasts a lifetime. Because as wounds are healed, other wounds continue to be inflicted. During the four-year process of writing *Wounded by God's People*, I have been wounded. Again and again. In fact, I've been wounded as severely as at any other time in my life. I have known, therefore, that God was allowing me to experience in a fresh way the insights that I have shared with you in these pages.

And He is continuing to teach me that living in my forgiveness from Him, and His for me, and mine for others, is a way of life.

In His faithfulness, God has brought people alongside who lifted me up during the writing process. While there is no room at the end of this book to name them all, I would like to specifically thank members of my Zondervan publishing team who have truly gone above and beyond what would have been required of their position to see this writing project through to a successful conclusion.

Cindy Lambert — because of significant writing delays, I was invited by Zondervan to return to Grand Rapids and present my vision for *Wounded by God's People* to my publishing team for a second time. They gave me their blessing, but when the team had exited the board room, Cindy, the interim publisher at that time, slipped over beside me, took me by the hand, and said she wanted to pray for me because she knew that it was going to be a difficult writing project. Her thoughtfulness that prompted her prayer and her sensitivity as she prayed have stayed with me. Thank you, Cindy, for lifting me up, and, in turn, I pray as you read this that you will be aware that our God is a prayer-hearing, prayer-answering God.

Sandy Vander Zicht has been my editor from the beginning of my time with Zondervan. She is excellent, strong, professional, and has several other books she has edited currently on the *New York Times* bestseller list. We have become friends. But for *Wounded by God's People*, she not only gave me the skill of her editorial pen, she gave me her heart. She poured herself into the process, getting much more involved, and to a much deeper level, than what was required or what I would have expected. This entire book, and I myself, have been lifted up as a result. Thank you, dear Sandy.

Dudley Delffs was the publisher at Zondervan who gave his blessing to my vision for this book when I first presented it. He has since left Zondervan to pursue other things, but when I was struggling with the second draft of the manuscript, I asked if he would help Sandy and me with the content editing. He did. With a kind, encouraging spirit, he gave me ideas, suggestions, criticism, and applause.

He pushed me way beyond what I would have written on my own. Thank you, Dudley, for lifting me up and out of where I was before you came alongside.

Londa Alderink headed up the marketing and design team that dreamed up the cover for *Wounded by God's People*. Her attentiveness to my suggestions, her hearing of my concerns, and her capturing of the essence of the book in the cover art lifted me up at the very end of the writing project, giving wind in my sails as I completed the manuscript. Thank you, Londa.

Scott McDonald, as the president of Zondervan, and *Tracy Danz*, as Zondervan's publisher of trade books, both went out of their way to meet with me on multiple occasions, giving me their blessing and encouragement. As a result, over the extended writing period, the support of the team was never in question. Without them, this book would not have been published. Thank you, Scott and Tracy.

Bob Hudson was the last person on my Zondervan team to touch the manuscript before it went into typesetting. He polished the words, corrected the verb tenses, checked the references, verified the quotes ... and did so with quiet and warm efficiency. Thank you, Bob. And thank you for sharing my love for *The Valley of Vision*.

Most of all, I want to thank Hagar's God, the Angel of the Lord, for fulfilling what He promised in Psalm 147:3: "He heals the broken-hearted and binds up their wounds."

Now my prayer is that you, dear reader, have been lifted up as a result of the combined efforts of all of us. May God bless you and bring you to the end of your healing journey.

Anne

Notes

Preface: Jesus Understands

1. Joshua 7.
2. John 1:11 NASB.
3. Matthew 9:3.
4. Matthew 9:34.
5. Matthew 12:14.
6. Matthew 22:15.
7. Matthew 26:3 – 4.
8. Matthew 26:57, 67.
9. Matthew 27:1 – 2, 26.
10. 1 Peter 2:23.
11. Hebrews 12:2 – 3.

Introduction: Healing Is a Journey

1. Anne Graham Lotz, *The Magnificent Obsession: Embracing the God-Filled Life* (Grand Rapids, Mich.: Zondervan, 2009).
2. Other than Jesus Christ, Abraham may be the greatest man ever to have lived in human history. Jews, Christians, and Muslims all look to him as their patriarch. And God called him "friend."

The Biblical Story of Hagar

1. *Ishmael* means "the Lord hears."
2. Genesis 12:14, 16; 13:1; 16:1 – 16; 21:1 – 21.

Chapter 1: Loved by God on the Periphery

1. Genesis 12:15.
2. Genesis 12:16.
3. Genesis 20:12.
4. Genesis 12:3.
5. Genesis 12:17.
6. Genesis 12:20.
7. Joshua 2, 6.
8. Joshua 2:10.
9. Joshua 2:11.
10. Joshua 2:11.
11. Joshua 6:15 – 23.
12. Romans 3:23.
13. Ephesians 1:7.
14. John 3:16; Romans 6:23.
15. John 17:3.
16. Revelation 3:20.
17. John 8:12; 10:27; 12:26.
18. And you are saved! If your cry was sincerely uttered, God has heard you. Right now, you are saved. He gives you His Word:

The Lord is near to all who call
    on him,
    to all who call on him in truth.
He fulfills the desires of those
    who fear him;
    he hears their cry and saves them.
        (Psalm 145:18 – 19)

Take God at His Word. He is a gentleman — He doesn't lie, He means what He says, and says what He means. If He says you're forgiven, you're forgiven (1 John 1:9; Ephesians 1:7). If He says you have eternal life, you have eternal life (John 3:16; Ephesians 1:13 – 14). If He says He will live in you, never to leave nor forsake you (Hebrews 13:5), then He lives in you right now in the person of the Holy Spirit, and He will never leave nor forsake you. If He says He loves you (Jeremiah 31:3), dear reader on the periphery, then He loves you! What He says is so! (Psalm 119:89).

Chapter 2: Life Is Hard

1. Galatians 5:17 – 21.
2. Romans 3:23; Jeremiah 17:9.
3. Genesis 13:4.
4. Genesis 14:22.
5. Genesis 12:1 – 3.
6. Genesis 15:2 – 6.
7. Genesis 13.

Chapter 3: The Cycle of Pain

1. Genesis 16:2.
2. Genesis 16:2, 4.
3. Genesis 2:24.
4. Genesis 16:4.
5. Genesis 16:5 – 6.
6. Matthew 5:22; some old manuscripts insert "But I tell you the truth, that anyone who is angry with his brother without cause will be subject to judgment."
7. 1 Samuel 1:6, 7, 15.
8. 1 Samuel 1:15 – 16.
9. 1 Samuel 1:18.
10. 1 Samuel 2:21.
11. 1 Samuel 2:1 – 10.
12. Genesis 16:6.
13. Genesis 16:6.

Chapter 4: The Believer in Exile

1. http://marquee.blogs.cnn.com/2010/07/30/anne-rice-leaves-christianity.

Chapter 5: God Cares

1. Psalm 5:1 – 3, 5 – 6, 8 – 9, 10, 11 – 12.
2. Genesis 16:7.
3. John 21:1 – 3.
4. Genesis 16:7.
5. Genesis 32:22 – 32.
6. Joshua 5:13 – 6:5.
7. Judges 6:11 – 12.
8. Psalm 139:7 – 10.

Chapter 6: Spiritual Blind Spots

1. Genesis 16:8.
2. Genesis 16:8.
3. Genesis 16:4.
4. Matthew 7:3 – 5.
5. Sylvia Gunter, *Prayer Portions* (Birmingham, Ala.: The Father's Business, 1995).
6. Genesis 16:9 – 10.
7. Genesis 16:13.
8. Genesis 16:5.
9. Genesis 16:15.
10. Acts 3:19.

Chapter 7: Wounding Hurts

1. John 15:1 – 2.

2. Hebrews 12:11.
3. Genesis 15:5.
4. Galatians 4:29.
5. Genesis 21:10.
6. Genesis 2:24; Matthew 19:4 – 6.
7. Genesis 21:11.
8. Genesis 21:12 – 13.
9. Genesis 21:14.
10. Isaiah 55:9.
11. Psalm 23:3.
12. Romans 8:29; John 15:8.
13. Isaiah 53:4 – 5, 10.
14. John 3:16.
15. 1 Peter 2:23; 1 John 3:16.
16. Hebrews 2:14; 1 Corinthians 15:55 – 57; Romans 3:25; Titus 2:15; John 14:1 – 3; Hebrews 2:10.
17. Luke 24:1 – 7.
18. John 17:5.
19. Ephesians 1:19 – 23.
20. Hebrews 12:2 – 3.

Chapter 8: Rejected by Them
1. Lamentations 2:11; 3:19 – 23.
2. John 1:11.

Chapter 9: Wandering in the Wilderness
1. Exodus 20:21.
2. Exodus 16:10.
3. Genesis 21:14.
4. Genesis 16:13.
5. Genesis 21:15.
6. Exodus 33:18.
7. Exodus 33:19; 34:6.
8. 2 Corinthians 1:3 – 4.
9. Job 12:13; Isaiah 55:8 – 9.
10. 2 Corinthians 12:9.

11. Exodus 15:26; Psalm 147:3; John 10:3 – 4, 11, 14.

Chapter 10: God Stands By
1. Genesis 12:8; 13:4; 18:16 – 33 are just three examples of Abraham's prayer life.
2. Genesis 12:7; 13:18.
3. Genesis 21:15 – 16.
4. Genesis 16:10.
5. The story is true, but Maria's name has been changed to protect her privacy. For other stories like hers, please read Tom Doyle's *Dreams and Visions: Is Jesus Awakening the Muslim World?* (Nashville: Thomas Nelson, 2012).
6. Jonah 2:2 – 7.
7. Mark 6:48.

Chapter 11: The Silence Is Broken
1. This is a wonderful description of God that was a hallmark phrase of the late Dr. T. E. Koshy, a mentor and friend to many, including my friend Joel Rosenberg.
2. Mother's car was fixed so that the damage was erased and it looked like new. And I did indeed become a better driver. I got my license at the age of sixteen, and to this day, at the age of sixty-five, I have never gotten a ticket. While I've been in some accidents, I have never caused another accident, for which I thank God! My father's encouraging and wise words to me have been proven true.
3. Genesis 17:1 – 22.
4. Genesis 17:23 – 27.

5. Genesis 18:13 – 14.

6. Genesis 18:20 – 33.

7. Genesis 20:1 – 18.

8. Genesis 12:14 – 20.

9. Genesis 21:17.

10. Genesis 21:17.

11. Genesis 21:17.

Chapter 12: A Stubborn Spirit

1. William Lobdell, *Losing My Religion: How I Lost My Faith Reporting on Religion in America and Found Unexpected Peace* (New York: HarperCollins, 2009).

2. Genesis 21:17.

3. Hebrews 13:5.

4. 1 Chronicles 16:34.

5. Isaiah 63:9.

6. Genesis 50:20.

7. Luke 1:37.

Chapter 13: The Turning Point

1. 1 Kings 19:1 – 21.

2. 1 Kings 19:7.

3. 1 Kings 19:9.

4. Genesis 21:17.

5. Isaiah 54:11 – 13 NASB (adapted). The noun *son* is plural in the original text. I took the liberty of hearing it in the singular, as God's word of comfort and encouragement to me about my own son.

6. Genesis 21:18.

7. John 19:26 – 27.

8. Luke 23:39 – 43.

9. Matthew 8:3.

10. Matthew 8:14 – 15.

11. Matthew 9:29.

12. Matthew 17:7.

Chapter 14: I Can See!

1. Genesis 21:19.

2. Exodus 17:3 – 6.

3. 2 Corinthians 1:3 – 4.

4. Genesis 21:19.

5. Genesis 21:18.

6. The prayers in this volume have also resonated in the heart of my younger brother, Ned. He read one of them at my mother's memorial service.

7. Arthur Bennett, ed., *The Valley of Vision: A Collection of Puritan Prayers and Devotions* (Edinburgh: Banner of Truth Trust, 1975), xxiv.

Chapter 15: Don't Look Back

1. Huckabee, Fox News, March 17, 2012.

2. Genesis 19:17.

3. Genesis 19:26.

4. Genesis 21:19.

5. Genesis 21:18.

6. Genesis 21:21.

7. Colossians 3:13.

8. Matthew 6:15.

9. C. S. Lewis, *God in the Dock* (Grand Rapids, Mich.: Eerdmans, 1972), 49.

10. Ephesians 4:32.

11. The story is true, but the name has been changed.

12. 1 John 3:16, 18, 23.

13. The story is true, but Jay's name has been changed to protect his privacy.

14. Luke 23:34.

15. Crawford Loritts is the senior pastor of Fellowship Bible Church in

Atlanta, Georgia, a frequent speaker at Promise Keepers, and one of the two men who join me in discussing revival in my video Bible-study curriculum, *Expecting to See Jesus.*

16. John 20:26 – 27.

17. Philippians 2:8 – 11; Revelation 5:6 – 14.

18. Ephesians 1:17 – 18.

Chapter 16: It's Time to Move On

1. And yes, I had followed that choice to forgive with sacrificial deeds.

2. John Ortberg, *Who Is This Man? The Unpredictable Impact of the Inescapable Jesus* (Grand Rapids, Mich.: Zondervan, 2012), 89.

3. Genesis 25:8 – 9.

4. While the story is true, David's name has been changed to protect his privacy.

5. Hebrews 4:15 – 16.

Conclusion: The End of the Healing Journey

1. Luke 15:13.

2. Romans 8:15; Galatians 4:6.

3. Jeremiah 29:11.

Epilogue: Quarried Deep

1. Romans 12:9, NKJV; James 5:8 – 9.

2. Galatians 6:17; 2:20; 2 Corinthians 12:7.

3. Philippians 3:10, 13 – 14.

4. Jesus used this very analogy in John 12:24 – 25 when He said, "I tell you the truth, unless a kernel of wheat falls to the ground and dies, it remains only a single seed. But if it dies, it produces many seeds. The man who loves his life will lose it, while the man who hates his life in this world will keep it for eternal life."

5. "The Deeps," from Arthur Bennett, ed., *The Valley of Vision: A Collection of Puritan Prayers and Devotions* (Edinburgh: Banner of Truth Trust, 2002), 134.

Also by Anne Graham Lotz

The Vision of His Glory

God's Story

Daily Light

Just Give Me Jesus

Heaven: My Father's House

Pursuing MORE of Jesus

Why? Trusting God When You Don't Understand

The Joy of My Heart

My Jesus Is ... Everything

The Magnificent Obsession

Heaven: God's Promise for Me

Expecting to See Jesus

Fixing My Eyes on Jesus

A Note to the Reader

After completing this book, if you need additional resources to help you dig deeper into God's Word, please contact Anne Graham Lotz through one of the following means:

AnGeL Ministries
5115 Hollyridge Drive
Raleigh, North Carolina 27612
919.787.6606
www.AnneGrahamLotz.com.
angelmin.info@angelministries.org

Share Your Thoughts

With the Author: Your comments will be forwarded to the author when you send them to *zauthor@zondervan.com*.

With Zondervan: Submit your review of this book by writing to *zreview@zondervan.com*.

Free Online Resources at
www.zondervan.com

Daily Bible Verses and Devotions: Enrich your life with daily Bible verses or devotions that help you start every morning focused on God. Visit www.zondervan.com/newsletters.

Free Email Publications: Sign up for newsletters on Christian living, academic resources, church ministry, fiction, children's resources, and more. Visit www.zondervan.com/newsletters.

Zondervan Bible Search: Find and compare Bible passages in a variety of translations at www.zondervanbiblesearch.com.

Other Benefits: Register to receive online benefits like coupons and special offers, or to participate in research.